Prayers from the Darkness

Prayers from the Darkness
The Difficult Psalms

Lyn Fraser

CHURCH PUBLISHING
New York

A catalog record for this book is available from the Library of Congress.

ISBN: 0-89869-500-7

Church Publishing, Incorporated
445 Fifth Avenue
New York, New York 10016

5 4 3 2 1

For my family

꒰ꔛ꒱

CONTENTS

↭

ACKNOWLEDGMENTS

To begin, I would like to thank the following individuals who have contributed to this book through the generous sharing of their stories and experiences: Georgia Adamson, Ken Arnold, Caroline Conway, Cathy DiPaola, Muzz Ebright, Brenda Fhuere, Mary Green, Suzanne Guinn, Jacqueline Hansen, Jane Heitman, Ora Houston, Sonya Ingwersen, Daphne Levey, Judith Liro, Julia Dorsey Loomis, Abbie Marschner, Hilary Martin, Mack Moore, Melanie Porter, Greg Rickel, Josie Rose, Patrick Sanders, Teri Schecter, Judy Schneider, and Beverly Williams-Hawkins.

I acknowledge with considerable appreciation Professor Donald S. Armentrout of the School of Theology, University of the South, for his support of my doctoral studies; and Professor Rebecca Wright for introducing me to the writings of Walter Brueggemann. At the Episcopal Seminary of the Southwest, I express appreciation for the enthusiastic encouragement of Professor Michael H. Floyd and his belief in the value of this work; and for the ideas and suggestions of Professor William S. Adams.

I am grateful to my aunt, Derby Quin Hirst, for introducing me to the work of Cynthia Shattuck, and to the community of St. James Episcopal Church in Austin, Texas, for allowing us to meet in person. Many months ago we met at a Sunday Eucharist and afterward had a brief discussion about my idea for this book. With her considerable expertise as an editor, her patience and insight during my seasons of disorientation, and her unwavering sense of the spiritual, Cynthia has helped me turn that idea into reality. It is also a pleasure to work with Amy Davis and Parul Parmer at Church Publishing.

There are many, many people in my church, writing, golfing, neighborhood, and good-friends communities whose names are not listed here but who have been tremendously supportive during the work on this book, and I am thankful for them.

My wonderful daughter Eleanor provides energy and inspiration in countless ways, often serving as the subject of my daily reflective writing on the psalms—including the difficult ones. I appreciate my brother Quin for his unwavering support of all my writing projects.

Finally, I would like to express enormous thanks to and thanksgiving for Reenie, who has read, commented upon, and generally encouraged all the words of the book (as well as many that were ultimately deleted); R.T.; Toot; and Addie Mae, whose Black Lab puppyhood coincided with the writing of the book, which means that she often chewed and sometimes consumed pages as fast as I could write them.

INTRODUCTION

Georgia, a hospice patient who was dying of A.L.S., told me one afternoon after many visits and conversations that she was angry at God for putting her in the situation in which her body was steadily deteriorating while her brain remained healthy and active. She was angry at God, really angry, for all she was losing and would lose. But she felt guilty about it. Knowing how much Georgia relied on the psalms as prayers and also appreciating her sense of humor, which by then I knew quite well, I told Georgia about the liturgical tradition in my church of chanting whatever psalm was appointed for a particular Sunday, and sang aloud from Psalm 63, "O God, you are my God, I seek you." Then I went on to explain that we had to chant whatever psalm was appointed, so we sometimes sang very sweetly about vindictive and angry things in the same lovely, lilting tune. I sang very sweetly from Psalm 68: "But God will shatter the heads of his enemies, the hairy crown of those who walk in their guilty ways." Georgia smiled. I sang from Psalm 79: "How long, O Lord? Will you be angry forever? Pour out your anger on the nations that do not know you." We both began to laugh, and Georgia chimed in with a few smiting and smashing verses of her own. She said she felt better about being mad, that it must be all right, given that God gets mad and so do the psalmists. There seemed to be great relief for Georgia in admitting her anger and expressing it in this way—honestly but with humor, both characteristics that fit her personality.

Following that conversation as well as others with members of the hospice staff and her family, Georgia was able to make decisions to refuse a respirator, feeding tube, and other life-extending measures, and she died peacefully in her sleep several months later. I know that the conversation stayed with her because in one of my last visits with her, I had put a damp washcloth on her forehead and thought she was asleep when she turned her head slightly toward me. She said, "Do you remember the time we sang those psalms?" and smiled. Georgia gracefully exemplified the hospice philosophy of healing without cure.

The book of Psalms in its entirety reflects a wholeness of human experience, individually and communally, in relation to God. But as the experience with Georgia vividly illustrates, to embrace only the appealing portions of the psalms in worship and prayer is to deny some of who we are as human beings and to block communication with God in the situations and circumstances when we most need it.

With their themes of anger, violence, vindication, and alienation, many psalms repel people because they feel that these expressions are in some way inappropriate or uncomfortable as prayers to God. They are the psalms that are rarely prayed in Sunday services, and when they are used it is often with difficult verses omitted. For similar reasons, these psalms are often avoided when we are praying by ourselves.

Why do we think it is necessary to clean up our prayers to God? Do we believe God will love us more or respond more positively to our prayers if we conceal our feelings of fury, hurt, vulnerability, self-pity, and loneliness? Perhaps we have difficulty, especially in the context of Jesus' teachings, expressing to God our hatred of enemies and the desire that our adversaries be punished and destroyed; or we think that if we avoid or deny certain thoughts and feelings, they don't exist or will go away; or we have some notion that prayers in church should only be about praise, joy, and thanksgiving. Perhaps we believe we know something about prayer that was somehow missed by the psalmists, Job, the Old Testament prophets, and Jesus Christ. In some sections of the Christian church, all verses of every psalm have been recited for centuries. As a devout Jew, Jesus prayed the psalms. Jesus taught us to love our enemies, but he raged against injustice, intolerance, and exclusivity, and he championed the cause of society's marginalized. The enemies Jesus referred to did not include such adversaries as addictions, gang violence, AIDS, crack babies, sexual abuse, depression, cancer, and racism. One explanation for the "psalms-sanitation" process offered by William L. Holladay in *The Psalms through Three Thousand Years* is simply that the modern church has a "tendency to bypass material with a negative import" (314), which many psalms certainly have. For the church to ignore that we have vindictive thoughts and feelings, unfortunately, does not make it so.

Returning to Georgia, another explanation that might be offered has to do with our expectations about prayer. Georgia admitted that she felt guilty about her anger, about emotions that she was reluctant to take to God because God was the cause of her ire. The change that ultimately occurred in response to Georgia's praying the psalms of anger had nothing whatsoever to do with her *external* circumstances—such as the possibility of "getting better." Her health was deteriorating in a process that would continue to worsen until she died, so no improvement in her physical condition was going to occur. The transformation that occurred for Georgia was *within*. (The concept of healing without cure is discussed more fully in chapter 3.) What changed was Georgia's attitude—toward her illness, her life within the confines of that illness, and God's role in all of that.

Psalms as Transformative

The purpose of this book is to help readers embrace more fully those psalms that have uncomfortable emotions and images. I would like to begin by making a case for these psalms, not with a list of reasons and arguments, but with seven stories that, like Georgia's, show the psalms' potential for healing in a range of pastoral circumstances.* As these experiences show, the portions of the psalms that many readers find offensive and inappropriate for worship are the very verses that enable some people to express emotions that are difficult to acknowledge, to pray to God out of these emotions, and to find a way forward toward healing.

Jim, the on-call chaplain at a Chicago area hospital, was called into the emergency room on a Sunday evening to visit Lila, a young woman who had just been raped and who had requested a chaplain. Jim felt at something of a loss. He was not a trained rape counselor, and even more difficult, he was a man with a woman who had been violated. When Jim arrived, Lila was in an E.R. cubicle with people screaming all around, adding to the nightmarish quality. She grabbed Jim's hand and started to cry, and for a few moments they just sat there. Lila said, "I just don't know where to go with this, with my anger. I don't know how to pray. I wanted to read the psalms, but they are all about praise and the goodness of God—except those awful ones that are so violent. Am I allowed to pray those awful things?" Jim assured her that she absolutely was, that the psalms are for all times, and this was a time to use those "awful" psalms. Together, they read Psalms 58 and 59 with verses asking in graphic detail for God's vengeance against the wicked and rescue for the innocent:

> The wicked go astray from the womb; they err from their birth, speaking lies.
> O God, break their teeth in their mouths; tear out the fangs of the young lions,
>   O Lord!
> Let them vanish like water that runs away; like grass let them be trodden
>   down and wither.
> Let them be like the snail that dissolves into slime; like the untimely birth that
>   never sees the sun.
> The righteous will rejoice when they see vengeance done;
>   they will bathe their feet in the blood of the wicked. (Ps. 58:3, 6–8, 10)**
> Deliver me from those who work evil; from the bloodthirsty save me.
> For no fault of mine, they run and make ready.
> Each evening they come back, howling like dogs and prowling about the city.
>   (Ps. 59:2, 4, 14)

Jim says that Lila was noticeably relieved to be encouraged to take her feelings to God—to pray about breaking the teeth of the enemy, who run

---

* These stories are based on factual situations with some names and locations changed to protect confidentiality.
** Psalm translations throughout the book, unless otherwise noted, are from the New Revised Standard Version.

about the city like howling dogs. She found it freeing to believe it was not wrong to want those things to happen to her attacker, expressed in a prayer to God. Lila was noticeably more relaxed after they read the psalms, and she was able to go ahead with the other things that needed to be done by the hospital staff.

Before this experience, Jim was one of those people who skipped over these unpleasant parts of the psalms when he read Scripture assigned from the Daily Office. He says that the experience with Lila was the very first time he saw clearly the wholeness of the psalms as a source of prayer.

✼

As a counselor at a veterans' hospital, Nan leads groups for the treatment of drug and alcohol abuse. She reported a major breakthrough for a Gulf War veteran, Ted, as a result of his studying Psalm 38. This particular psalm was one of the many resources Nan had suggested, and she was delighted when Ted announced that he had finally found something in Scripture he could relate to. He identified with the psalmist's vivid descriptions of a condition remarkably similar to Ted's own in battling his addiction: "I am utterly spent and crushed; I groan because of the tumult in my heart" (v. 8). But Ted also had feelings of shame and guilt:

> There is no health in my bones because of my sin.
> For my iniquities have gone over my head; they weigh like a burden too heavy for me.
> My wounds grow foul and fester because of my foolishness. (Ps. 38:3–5)

He shared as well the psalmist's bitter description of the response of others: "My friends and companions stand aloof from my affliction, and my neighbors stand far off" (v. 11). Getting to the point of acknowledging these feelings represented important progress, as did beginning to take some responsibility for his circumstance. Ted recognized the movement at the end of the psalm, the turning to God for help: "Do not forsake me, O Lord; O my God, do not be far from me" (v. 21). He admitted he was "not there yet," but expressed hope that he could build toward the level of trust in God expressed in the psalm.

✼

After a tumultuous period of strife within a small parish, the priest left to accept another position. Some members left the congregation to attend another church, and the remaining community felt abandoned, alienated, and in disarray, wondering what to do next. In an effort to rebuild community, one of the parish members, Mary Edna, decided to host Sunday evening soup suppers to listen to a series of taped sermons and discuss the content. About twenty members of the congregation regularly attended the gatherings over ten months. One of the sermons they heard and discussed was based on verses 5 and 6 from Psalm 120:

> Woe is me, that I am an alien in Meshech,
> that I must live among the tents of Kedar.
> Too long have I had my dwelling among those who hate peace. (vv. 5–6)

According to the sermon, Meshech and Kedar represented for the speaker of this psalm not only places (the names of nomadic tribes far from Jerusalem), but a state of mind. These tribes were noted for their hostility and ferocity, and the psalmist—in the sermon account—is recognizing the need for a change in state of mind, for a new way of looking at life that reflects peace and reconciliation. The discussion that followed that evening's sermon helped move the community toward needed reconciliation and healing among its members and the eventual agreement on the calling of a new priest. The church members relating this story attribute the positive movement to equal parts psalm, discussion, and Mary Edna's soup.

ᘐ

With his background in the Hispanic Roman Catholic tradition, Carlos was new to the Episcopal Church and wasn't sure he wanted to be there. He asked Martha, the priest who was leading the Discovery Class, what was "fair" to ask in prayer. He had been taught a lot of rules about religious behavior and decorum and wanted to know what was appropriate to say to God. Martha suggested he read the entire book of Psalms, which he did. When they met to discuss his reading, Carlos expressed amazement at the range of what people in the past had communicated to God, especially some of the psalms that he had previously considered to be off-limits, such as Psalm 55, with verses that are not only self-pitying—"I am troubled in my complaint" (v. 2) and "My heart is in anguish within me" (v. 4)—but also which complain about the hurt inflicted by a close friend:

> It is not enemies who taunt me—I could bear that;
> it is not adversaries who deal insolently with me—I could hide from them.
> But it is you, my equal, my companion, my familiar friend, with whom I kept
>   pleasant company;
> we walked in the house of God with the throng. (vv. 12–14)

Carlos said that such psalms freed him up just to pray and not worry any more about what was "fair." He became a member of the church, and his extemporaneous prayers are said to be wonderfully creative.

ᘐ

Grieving the death of her young husband, Janet had also to suffer from unpleasant treatment by his family. At the suggestion of her spiritual director, Janet was reading psalms of struggle. On one of the horrible nights when she was exhausted but could not fall asleep because the stress and misery of the day whirled through her mind, she read Psalm 4, struck by its question: "How long, you people, shall my honor suffer shame?" (v. 2), and comforted by the eventual answer, "I will both lie down and sleep in peace; for you alone, O Lord, make me lie down in safety" (v. 8). Janet says that on many subsequent nights, this psalm was both prayer and mantra. "In repeating it, I knew its truth, I knew I could let go and let the One in charge watch over everything. And I could sleep, and sleep well."

⁍

Three years after coming to the church as an assistant in education and pastoral care, Meredith assumed an increasing share of responsibilities as her immediate superior suffered from heart disease. When it finally became apparent that her boss would have to retire, Meredith and others in the congregation assumed that she would obtain the position. Many members of the church wrote letters of support, but the denomination's regional administrator, who had the final say, brought in someone from outside the congregation for the job. Feeling mistreated and undervalued, Meredith considered resigning immediately but decided to take the problem to her weekly prayer group, whose members were also extremely upset about the decision and having their views ignored. After a few minutes of silence, the group decided to read together Psalm 109, which includes the verses:

> In return for my love they accuse me, even while I make prayer for them.
> So they reward me evil for good, and hatred for my love.
> May his days be few; may another seize his position.
> May the creditor seize all that he has; may strangers plunder the fruits of his toil.
> May there be no one to do him a kindness, nor anyone to pity his orphaned children.
> I am an object of scorn to my accusers; when they see me, they shake their heads.
> Let them curse, but you will bless. (vv. 45, 8, 11–12, 25, 28)

The praying of the psalm with its verses expressing a desire for specific acts of vengeance provided an essential venting for their feelings of outrage and injustice, and a release of their hostile feelings toward the administrator. Meredith and the others were able to discuss the situation more calmly and to move on with their involvement in the congregation and denomination.

⁍

On one of the Sundays shortly after September 11, 2001, the priest in my parish effectively used the appointed psalm, Psalm 37, not just as the text of the sermon but as the entire sermon—by first reading it from the perspective of American citizens and then turning the psalm on its head and reading it from the perspective of our so-called enemies:

> The wicked draw the sword and bend their bows to bring down the poor and needy,
> to kill those who walk uprightly;
> their sword shall enter their own heart, and their bows shall be broken.
> For the arms of the wicked shall be broken, but the LORD upholds the righteous. (vv. 14, 15, 17)

Most of us were still in shock after the terrorist attacks, but this reading of the psalm woke us up as a worshiping community to alternate points of view about what had happened, raising obvious questions about who are the righteous and who are the wicked, and who are the poor and needy, and whose tongues are speaking justice.

From Disorientation to New Orientation

What the people in all of these stories have in common is a profound sense of *disorientation*, triggered by some sort of upheaval in their lives: terminal illness, violation, addiction, grief, alienation, distrust, terror, injustice. When we are disoriented, we lose our sense of place, our sense of direction. Each of the examples demonstrates an instance in which one or more of the psalms helps turn a key, leading to release and the beginning of movement out of a situation in which movement is essential for recovery. Old Testament scholar Walter Brueggemann has developed a grouping for the psalms in a way that reflects this progression in our lives by using themes of orientation, disorientation, and new orientation. Brueggemann's approach in *The Message of the Psalms* is explored more fully in chapter 1.

Psalms of disorientation acknowledge our periods of suffering by expressing anguish, disarray, and dislocation, both individually and communally. The examples illustrate the transformative power of these psalms of suffering for pastoral care situations (Georgia, Lila, Ted, Carlos), in liturgical settings (Mary Edna's church community and my own parish after 9/11), in solitary prayer (Janet), and in small-group prayer (Meredith). The chapters that follow explore and develop ways in which psalms of disorientation can help promote, as they did in each of the stories, the desired shift toward a new orientation, where light breaks through the darkness and we are able to restore balance and order to our lives after an experience of alienation and disequilibrium. We emerge singing thanksgiving and God's praise, but with the new sounds of Psalms 96 and 98: "O sing to the LORD a new song."

The initial two chapters of the book consider the church's approach to psalms of disorientation: what we are missing as worshipers by avoiding such psalms in liturgy, how and why psalms of suffering and struggle have been used historically in prayer and worship, and some of the specific ways in which these psalms could be more fully integrated into worship settings and the life of the church. We then turn to an exploration of these psalms in a variety of pastoral care situations, including death and bereavement; illness and aging; major transitions, such as divorce, the loss of employment, and geographic dislocation; special circumstances, such as ministries to those who are incarcerated; and ministries to adolescents. The concluding chapter discusses the relevance of these psalms to our personal prayer lives during times of anguish, anxiety, and alienation.

The intent throughout the book is to demonstrate how an individual or corporate experience is related to the content and themes of the psalms, and how the feelings associated with our times of struggle and sorrow might be prayerfully expressed through a psalm, always with an awareness of the ebb and flow between anguish and hope, and between despair and trust in God, with movement toward healing, a renewed sense of wholeness, and new orientation. Ultimately, the central theme of this book is that the psalmists make their own strong case for incorporating these psalms into corporate worship and personal prayer life, by doing exactly that. At times of despair in their personal or communal lives, the psalmists take their expressions of suffering to God in faith.

PART ONE

Corporate Worship

〜

CHAPTER ONE

Yours Is the Day, Yours Also the Night
The Difficult Psalms

Some psalms are never a part of Sunday worship. Among those we do not hear on Sundays are psalms with such unsavory themes as the desire for vindication ("Let ruin come on them unawares," Ps. 35:8), the violation of sacred spaces ("The enemy has destroyed everything in the sanctuary," Ps. 74:3), mistreatment by friends ("You have caused my companions to shun me," Ps. 88:8), acute isolation ("I am like a lonely bird on the housetop," Ps. 102:7), and our own mortality ("You have made my days a few handbreadths, and my lifetime is as nothing in your sight," Ps. 39:5).

More commonly, we chant, pray, or read responsively about joy ("Therefore my heart is glad, and my soul rejoices," Ps. 16:9), blessings ("I will bless the LORD at all times," Ps. 34:1), the wonders of God's creation ("O LORD, how manifold are your works! In wisdom you have made them all; the earth is full of your creatures" (Ps. 104:24), and thanksgivings ("I give you thanks, O LORD, with my whole heart," Ps. 138:1). If we consider the psalms to be integral to our lives of faith through worship, however, *all* of these voices need to be heard because they reflect important aspects of how things actually are—in our lives, in our world, and within the church itself.

Well over two thousand years ago the psalmists related their personal and communal experiences of spirituality, collected as the book of Psalms. The psalms provide a major source in the Old Testament of the personal voice: humans speaking directly to God, rather than God speaking to humans or humans addressing one another. This body of work remains an incomparable spiritual resource in part because the psalmists' beliefs and feelings are much the same ones that we live with on a daily basis in the twenty-first century. Whatever our current condition—from the darkness of despair, grief, alienation, and anger to the brightness of joy, delight, praise, and thanksgiving—the psalmists invite us to honest and direct communication with God without holding anything back.

Much of what the psalmists express is not pleasant. The psalmists whine and complain. They are angry, bitter, and frustrated. They bargain and manipulate. They have crises and confrontations with neighbors, friends, and enemies. They grieve and moan. They are scared and insecure and self-pitying. They are spiteful and vindictive when things don't go their way. But they also embrace paradox, acknowledging that lightness and darkness can coexist in our lives, that God can be both present and absent. Even when sinking in deep mire where there is seemingly no foothold, they express their faith in God.

The psalms were written for a culture quite different from ours. C. S. Lewis, writing about the "cursing" psalms in *Reflections on the Psalms,* reminds us that the psalmists "lived in a world of savage punishments, of massacre and violence, of blood sacrifice. . . . And of course, too, we are far more subtle than they in disguising our ill will from others and from ourselves" (25). In spite of—and in some ways because of—differences in time and place, the psalms embody a transforming power by providing access to the psalmists' personal expressions of thoughts and feelings as they experience a living God. Their openness and honesty reflect an over-whelming trust in God.

Those Awful Ones

When Jim told me the story in the introduction about helping Lila, the young woman who had been raped, he said that she referred to some psalms as "those awful ones." Of course, I knew right away what psalms she meant. Lila is not alone in referring to some of the psalms with this and other similarly negative terms. They are the psalms, such as those cited in the introduction and at the beginning of this chapter, that readers find difficult to read and hear. They are *awful,* in the sense of being unpleasant, appalling, dreadful, and fearsome. Over the history of the English language, however, "awful" is one of the many words that has changed in meaning. When James II first saw St. Paul's Cathedral he called it, among other things, "awful," by which he meant that it was "deserving of awe" (Bryson 78). So these psalms *are* awful from several perspectives, but they are also more than awful.

One term for the body of psalms that I am going to use throughout the book is based on the work of Old Testament scholar and theologian Walter Brueggemann. In *The Message of the Psalms,* Brueggemann presents a scheme for categorizing the psalms in a way that reflects our life process by using themes of orientation, disorientation, and new orientation. An essential understanding is that life is not static; we *move* from one situation to another, changing and being changed. Brueggemann suggests that the life of faith, as expressed through the psalms, reflects that dynamic process. We move out of settled orientation into seasons of disorientation, and from disorientation into times of new orientation, where we are surprised by new gifts from God and experience a fresh sense of coherence. This progression applies both communally—to families, groups, organizations, congregations, a nation, the world—and to each of us as individuals.

Psalms of *orientation* reflect our seasons of well-being. These psalms articulate joy, goodness, delight, and order; they recognize and celebrate God's word, God's reliability, and God's creation. An example is Psalm 8, a psalm of creation that articulates God's overriding majesty while conveying security for humankind in a well-ordered creation where humans have authority, slightly below God, over the works of God's hands. As a border, the psalm begins and ends with the same doxology verse, praising God.

Orientation: Psalm 8

O LORD, our Sovereign, how majestic is your name in all the earth!

You have set your glory above the heavens. Out of the mouths of babes and infants
you have founded a bulwark because of your foes, to silence the enemy and the avenger.

When I look at your heavens, the work of your fingers, the moon and the stars that you established;
what are human beings that you are mindful of them, mortals that you care for them?

Yet you have made them a little lower than God, and crowned them with glory and honor.
You have given them dominion over the works of your hands; you have put all things
under their feet,
all sheep and oxen, and also the beasts of the field,
the birds of the air, and the fish of the sea, whatever passes along the paths of the seas.

O LORD, our Sovereign, how majestic is your name in all the earth!

Psalms of *disorientation* acknowledge periods of alienation, despair, and suffering, evoking emotions of anger, resentment, vengeance, self-pity, fear, shame, hostility, and grief. The psalms of disorientation express anguish, disarray, and alienation from God. Psalm 6, for example, is a personal lament.

Disorientation: Psalm 6

O LORD, do not rebuke me in your anger, or discipline me in your wrath.
Be gracious to me, O LORD, for I am languishing;
O LORD, heal me, for my bones are shaking with terror.
My soul also is struck with terror, while you, O LORD—how long?

Turn, O LORD, save my life; deliver me for the sake of your steadfast love.
For in death there is no remembrance of you; in Sheol who can give you praise?

I am weary with my moaning; every night I flood my bed with tears; I drench my couch with my weeping.
My eyes waste away because of grief; they grow weak because of all my foes.

Depart from me, all you workers of evil, for the LORD has heard the sound of
my weeping.
The LORD has heard my supplication; the LORD accepts my prayer.
All my enemies shall be ashamed and struck with terror; they shall turn back,
and in a moment be put to shame.

In a lament, whether personal or communal, the psalmist typically makes
a personal plea to God ("O LORD"); describes specific complaints ("languishing," "struck with terror," "weary with my moaning," "eyes waste
away"; lists the actions needed by God ("save my life," "deliver me");
explains why God should intervene ("for the sake of your steadfast love");
offers something in return for God's help (praise); and indicates that God
has heard the prayer ("the Lord has heard the sound of my weeping. The
Lord has heard my supplication; the Lord accepts my prayer"). The
psalmists are masterful bargainers; consider the psalmist's question: how
can I praise you if I'm in Sheol?

Psalms of *new orientation* affirm the overwhelming new gifts of God when
joy breaks through the despair, light through the darkness. These psalms
(such as Psalm 30, which is a song of thanks to God for rescue) often
include not only a statement of the problem but also its resolution, leading
to celebration, praise, and thanksgiving. Scholars believe that this psalm
may be associated with the Feast of Hanukkah, celebrating the restoration
of worship in the Temple in 164 B.C. (Craven and Harrelson 776).

New Orientation: Psalm 30

I will extol you, O LORD, for you have drawn me up, and did not let my foes
rejoice over me.
O LORD my God, I cried to you for help, and you have healed me.
O LORD, you brought up my soul from Sheol, restored me to life from among
those gone down to the Pit.

Sing praises to the LORD, O you his faithful ones, and give thanks to his holy
name.
For his anger is but for a moment; his favor is for a lifetime.
Weeping may linger for the night, but joy comes with the morning.

As for me, I said in my prosperity, "I shall never be moved." By your favor,
O Lord, you had established me as a strong mountain; you hid your face;
I was dismayed.

To you, O LORD, I cried, and to the Lord I made supplication: "What profit is
there in my death, if I go down to the Pit? Will the dust praise you? Will
it tell of your faithfulness?
Hear, O LORD, and be gracious to me! O LORD, be my helper!"

You have turned my mourning into dancing; you have taken off my sackcloth
and clothed me with joy, so that my soul may praise you and not be silent.
O LORD my God, I will give thanks to you forever.

All three of these categories of psalms are integral to the wholeness of the Psalter. While this book concentrates on psalms of disorientation for use in prayer and worship, it is with a keen awareness of their relationship to the other categories. In Psalm 8 (orientation), the psalmist celebrates the orderliness of God's creation and the marvelous place of humans in that order. From a contrasting life situation, the speaker in Psalm 6 (disorientation) languishes in grief, desperate for healing; this psalm flows between anguish and faith in God, expressed here in verses such as God's hearing the sound of weeping and accepting the psalmist's prayer. In Psalm 30 (new orientation), the speaker has emerged from the darkness and acknowledges with praise and thanksgiving God's help and healing; the desperate cry from the Pit of disorientation is answered, turning mourning into dancing.

When we are mired in a period of disequilibrium, we want to get out of it; the speaker in Psalm 6 raises the very human question of how long will this situation last. The grieving journey is an example of the movements we make in this process. When we experience a major loss—such as the loss of a loved one from death, the loss of a family unit from divorce, the loss of employment, the loss of a relationship, the loss of a pet, the loss of vitality from aging—we are thrust from relative orientation into disorientation, the severity of which depends upon the nature and circumstances of the loss. We are in the Pit. Grieving in a healthy way enables us to move on, although not in a linear way, to reach a place in our lives where we can reinvest energy into living rather than in having our lives overwhelmed by the grief, even though the loss is always a part of us. The grieving process, however, involves *grieving*. When the psalmists experience loss, they neither deny nor avoid the grief. Rather, they shout out their feelings and symptoms, vividly expressing every nuance of their situation, and they do so over and over again, like the speaker in Psalm 6: *I am languishing. I am weary with my moaning. I flood my bed with tears. My eyes waste away because of grief.* (Chapter 3 of this book offers further discussion and examples of how these psalms of sorrow are helpful in the grieving process.)

The psalmists draw continuously on their relationship with God, pleading for help and deliverance, with the objective of moving through and out of the darkness. Ellen F. Davis writes in *Getting Involved with God, Rediscovering the Old Testament* that "the Psalms teach us that profound change happens always in the presence of God. Over and over they attest to the reality that when we open our minds and hearts fully to God . . . we open ourselves, whether we know it or not, to the possibility of being transformed beyond our imagining" (5).

The stories in the introduction to the book show examples of situations in which psalms of disorientation help some one or some group—not in the sense of "Read a psalm and *poof*, all is well again," but in the sense of helping to shift toward new orientation. My hospice patient Georgia was able to make important decisions that affected her dying process. Lila, the rape victim, could go forward with needed treatment. Ted, the young man in the drug and alcohol abuse treatment program, had a breakthrough in the treatment of his addiction. The church community moved toward reconciliation. Carlos, the newcomer to the church, was released from worry about what was "fair" to pray. Janet, in her grief and strife, found a way to lie down and sleep in peace. Meredith and her supporters could continue to work in the church. The psalmists' intimate, honest expressions to God contributed to *positive* movement, a notion that represents a radical departure from the psalm-sanitation theory that such psalms mire us in negativity.

The psalms classified as psalms of disorientation include personal and communal laments as well as other psalms that reflect sorrow and struggle.

Psalms of Disorientation

Psalm 3	Psalm 35	Psalm 60	Psalm 88
Psalm 4	Psalm 38	Psalm 61	Psalm 90
Psalm 5	Psalm 39	Psalm 64	Psalm 94
Psalm 6	Psalm 42	Psalm 69	Psalm 102
Psalm 7	Psalm 43	Psalm 70	Psalm 109
Psalm 10	Psalm 44	Psalm 71	Psalm 120
Psalm 12	Psalm 49	Psalm 73	Psalm 123
Psalm 13	Psalm 50	Psalm 74	Psalm 126
Psalm 17	Psalm 51	Psalm 77	Psalm 130
Psalm 22	Psalm 54	Psalm 79	Psalm 137
Psalm 25	Psalm 55	Psalm 80	Psalm 140
Psalm 26	Psalm 56	Psalm 81	Psalm 141
Psalm 28	Psalm 57	Psalm 83	Psalm 142
Psalm 31	Psalm 58	Psalm 85	Psalm 143
Psalm 32	Psalm 59	Psalm 86	

These categories are not rigid, and someone else might come up with a slightly different list. There are also mixed psalms that are not included in the list but which contain elements of disorientation in some verses. These 59 psalms make up almost 40 percent of the book of Psalms. It is interesting to note that among the first 10 psalms in the book of Psalms, 6 are psalms of disorientation. Old Testament scholar J. Clinton McCann writes, "If the psalms teach us anything, it is that we have the license to hurt, to doubt, to scream in agony, as did the Psalmists, as did Job, as did Jeremiah, as did Jesus himself" (77). Perhaps the editors who selected and collected the 150 psalms more than two thousand years ago knew something about human nature!

Psalms of Disorientation in Corporate Worship

Lectionaries have been used since the fourth century to provide a table of readings from Scripture based on the church calendar. The *Revised Common Lectionary* (RCL), which is followed by many Protestant denominations in the United States and abroad, offers a three-year cycle of readings from Scripture for use in worship services on Sundays and major feast days, including Christmas, Holy Name, Epiphany, Ash Wednesday, Holy Week, Easter Vigil, Ascension, and Thanksgiving. Similar three-year reading cycles are provided in the Lectionary of the Episcopal *Book of Common Prayer* and the *Lectionary for Mass* of the Roman Catholic Church.

Denominations Using the Revised Common Lectionary (RCL)

In the United States of America, the Revised Common Lectionary (RCL) has been adopted for use by the following denominations:

American Baptist Church	Presbyterian Church USA
Christian Church (Disciples of Christ)	United Church of Christ
Christian Reformed Church in North America	United Methodist Church
Evangelical Lutheran Church in America	

The Seventy-third General Convention of the Episcopal Church USA called for a period of extensive study beginning in Advent 2000, with selected congregations using the RCL, as a step leading to full adoption. The Seventy-fourth General Convention of the Episcopal Church USA adopted a resolution that permits but does not require use of the RCL.

The RCL is used outside of the United States in Australia, Canada, Denmark, Estonia, Finland, France, Great Britain, Iceland, Japan, Korea, Melanesia, Netherlands, New Zealand, Papua New Guinea, Polynesia, South Africa, Sweden, and Venezuela (Episcopal Church).

More than 70 percent of the psalms used in the three-year scripture reading cycle of the *Revised Common Lectionary* are psalms with themes either of orientation or new orientation. This percentage is even higher for congregations using Episcopal and Roman Catholic lectionaries. The *Lutheran Book of Worship* provides the text of 122 psalms in its combined prayer book and hymnal; of the 28 psalms that are omitted, 18 are psalms of disorientation. While we do not totally eliminate all psalms of disorientation, they are not as frequently a part of the Scripture used in Sunday worship as are the other two categories. *A New Zealand Prayer Book*, which also omits verses and entire portions of these psalms, offers the baldest explanation: "Some verses of the psalms are not suitable for use in the corporate worship of the Church" (*New Zealand* 195).

The *Revised Common Lectionary* includes a total of 105 psalms in its three-year cycle; most of the psalms that are never appointed are psalms of disorientation. For the numerous denominations in the United States and abroad using the *Revised Common Lectionary*, many psalms such as those cited at the beginning of the chapter are thus never a part of worship. Historian William L. Holladay has closely analyzed the psalm texts that are omitted from the Roman Catholic Liturgy of the Hours, which contains patterns of avoidance similar to other lectionaries. He concludes that of the 22 psalms with all or some verses omitted, 14 are individual laments and 4 are laments of the community. Of the others, one ends with a plea for help; one offers thanksgiving after battle; and another proclaims the psalmist's innocence. All of the omissions include portions of psalms that refer to the psalmists' enemies, which are assumed also to be God's enemies (310). Somewhat humorously, Holladay points out the pope's explanation in 1970 for the omission of psalms and verses that are harsh in tone: "Parts of the Psalms that did not seem offensive to reciters who only half understood them in Latin are now to be omitted when the reciters hear what they really mean in their own language" (304–5). The purpose of a lectionary, well articulated by Eugene Brand, secretary for ecumenical relationships and worship of the Lutheran World Federation, is to "unfold the full sweep of God's revelation, not avoiding the hard words. If properly designed, a Lectionary keeps the Church from the ever-present danger of domesticating the scriptures" (Brand ix). But as Episcopal divinity professor Ivan T. Kaufman points out, available lectionaries, unfortunately, do not measure up if the laments of the Psalter are considered to be part of God's whole design (67).

Of the psalms of disorientation that are used in the *Revised Common Lectionary*, many are concentrated in the period from Palm Sunday through Holy Saturday, and those that are appointed for Sundays often have difficult verses omitted. When these verses are left out, the nature of the psalm actually changes so that the psalm is no longer a psalm of disorientation.

Psalm 25, for example, is a personal lament that is appointed four times in the lectionary cycle, but in each instance, only the first verses are used (e.g., "To you, O Lord, I lift up my soul." "Lead me in your truth and teach me, for you are the God of my salvation; for you I wait all day long." vv. 1, 5). Eliminated are the following personal cries to God for help from one who is alone and in misery:

> Turn to me and be gracious to me, for I am lonely and afflicted.
> Relieve the troubles of my heart, and bring me out of my distress.
> Consider my affliction and my trouble, and forgive all my sins.
> Consider how many are my foes, and with what violent hatred they hate me.
> O guard my life, and deliver me; do not let me be put to shame, for I take
> refuge in you. (vv. 16–20)

Psalm 85 is another disquieting psalm that is appointed four times in the lectionary cycle. On all but one of these occasions, verses are omitted, such as the following:

> Restore us again, O God of our salvation, and put away your indignation toward us.
> Will you be angry with us forever? Will you prolong your anger to all generations?
> Will you not revive us again, so that your people may rejoice in you? (vv. 4–6)

The communal lament of a nation in danger is converted into an announcement of peace and prosperity for those who turn to God:

> Surely his salvation is at hand for those who fear him, that his glory may dwell in our land.
> Steadfast love and faithfulness will meet; righteousness and peace will kiss each other.
> Faithfulness will spring up from the ground, and righteousness will look down from the sky.
> The LORD will give what is good, and our land will yield its increase.
> Righteousness will go before him, and will make a path for his steps. (vv. 9–13)

As a result of the editing, we eliminate the psalm's context and in the process "lose a model for lamenting over our own nation in hope of insight about how we might turn to God and find consolation" (Kaufman 74). Psalm 85's missing content, together with Psalm 74 (a communal lament that is never appointed), are especially appropriate in the aftermath of terrorists' destruction on September 11:

> Direct your steps to the perpetual ruins; the enemy has destroyed everything in the sanctuary.
> Your foes have roared within your holy place; they set up their emblems there.
> At the upper entrance they hacked the wooden trellis with axes.
> And then, with hatchets and hammers, they smashed all its carved work.
> They set your sanctuary on fire; they desecrated the dwelling place of your name, bringing it to the ground. They said to themselves, "We will utterly subdue them"; they burned all the meeting places of God in the land.
> Have regard for your covenant, for the dark places of the land are full of the haunts of violence. (Ps. 74:3–8, 20)

In response to 9/11, we participated as a nation in public prayers—communal laments—for our country and our people, for the thousands of lives lost and the families of those who died. As a nation, too, we responded by creating endless ruins in Afghanistan and Iraq, bombing and destroying, maiming and wounding and killing. We laid waste to other nations' sanctuaries. The quotation in Psalm 74, "We will utterly subdue them," could well be an evening news sound bite from the political leaders of many countries around the world. Our nation's response to violence has been violence and more violence. We are learning in this process that to many around the world, we are the enemy. What has been destroyed is something much broader and deeper than what can be represented by a physical place, even a sacred one. The psalms offer hope, but not in isolation. Events on and since September 11, 2001, the tsunami disaster in Asia, and the tragedy of Hurricane Katrina have emphasized the relevance of these communal laments to our own nation and have perhaps opened our ears more fully to the same prayers being said around the world.

As Brueggemann writes, "It is a curious fact that the church has, by and large, continued to sing songs of orientation in a world increasingly experienced as disoriented." It is his view that this action of the church is "less an evangelical defiance guided by faith, and much more a frightened, numb denial and deception that does not want to acknowledge or experience the disorientation of life" (*Message 51*). Singing regularly the psalms of disorientation would require that the church admit how things actually are with human beings, the world, the environment, and the church itself.

It is interesting, too, that the only psalms of suffering appointed in the *Revised Common Lectionary* during the seasons of Christmas and Epiphany (covering the period from the day after Christmas through Ash Wednesday) have verses omitted, eliminating the portions relating to disorientation. Psalm 71, for example, is appointed in the RCL during Epiphany, but using only the first six verses, leaving out "So even to old age and gray hairs, O God, do not forsake me. . . . You who have made me see many troubles and calamities will revive me again; from the depths of the earth you will bring me up again" (vv. 18, 20). This seems an especially striking incongruity between what the church is singing and what people are experiencing because these seasons of the church year are times marked by considerable societal disequilibrium, the so-called winter blues.

Grief support needs are also strong during this time in part because the winter months are the period of the year in the United States when more deaths occur than in any other season (National Center for Health Statistics), and also because acute grief is often triggered by "special" days such as Christmas, New Year's, and Valentine's Day. These potentially difficult seasons are obvious times when some psalms of pain and grief would be relevant to our life's rhythms.

Into the Light

There is no question that these psalms are difficult in the sense of challenging a worshiper with content that encompasses many thoughts, experiences, and feelings that we would rather not have and that we would prefer not to admit having. But we do have them. The psalmists provide a model, in fact, of what to do with such feelings—by taking them to God in prayer. Such prayer carries with it a responsibility as well. We are praying in good faith to God rather than acting on feelings such as the desire to harm others.

The "cursing psalms," according to L. Gregory Jones, dean of Duke University's Divinity School, are indispensable for individual spiritual health as well as for maintaining or restoring the health of the church (40). Instead of repressing or ignoring feelings of rage and bitterness in the face of injustice and betrayal, we should express them in corporate worship, engaging with God as we do so, and the psalmists provide us with a ready vocabulary of appropriate prayer. They communicate an understanding of faith that is intensely personal, but not private.

What also is evident in each of the same psalms that began the chapter is that the psalmist does not expect to be left in the dark. Along with the desire for revenge in Psalm 35 is a prayer for those who are vulnerable: "You deliver the weak from those too strong for them, the weak and needy from those who despoil them" (v. 10). There is vast destruction in Psalm 74, but also acknowledgment of God's creation, which includes both dark and light: "Yours is the day, yours also the night; you established the luminaries and the sun. You have fixed all the bounds of the earth; you made summer and winter" (vv. 16–17). Friends are unkind in Psalm 88, but the speaker is not left helpless: "O LORD, God of my salvation" (v. 1). From a place of extreme isolation in Psalm 102, the psalmist relies on the constancy of God: "but you are the same, and your years have no end. The children of your servants shall live secure; their offspring shall be established in your presence" (vv. 27–28). Facing mortality in Psalm 39, the psalmist asks, "And now, O Lord, what do I wait for? My hope is in you" (v. 7). Each of these psalms reflects the hope or possibility or actuality of movement out of a place that is desperate and unstable.

Lutheran theologian Gail Ramshaw even writes that in times such as ours, joy as our perpetual emotive stance is "naïve or selfish or fraudulent" because "secret sorrow, massive injustice, and the experience of abandonment are everywhere." She believes that we need to find ways to lament in corporate liturgy, and that by lamenting communally, we do so as shared witnesses to the resurrection (317, 320).

The power of these psalms of lament for liturgical prayer was indirectly but strongly affirmed by the participants in a recent workshop that I led on the psalms.

As part of our group process, I passed out individual copies of Psalm 86, a personal lament that reads, in part:

Incline your ear, O Lord, and answer me, for I am poor and needy.
Preserve my life, for I am devoted to you; save your servant who trusts in you;
You are my God; be gracious to me, O Lord, for to you do I cry all day long.
For you are great and do wondrous things; you alone are God.
O God, the insolent rise up against me; a band of ruffians seeks my life, and
    they do not set you before them.
But you, O Lord, are a God merciful and gracious, slow to anger and abounding
    in love and faithfulness.

Show me a sign of your favor, so that those who hate me may see it and be
   put of shame, because
you, Lord, have helped me and comforted me. (vv. 1–3, 10, 14–15, 17)

I asked the participants to read the psalm silently to themselves, which they did, and then we discussed it. Our discussion was relatively somber, with a few comments about the psalmist's "self-pitying tone" and "selfishness" in contrast to God's greatness. I then asked the group to read the psalm out loud, in unison, and that's when the conversation took off. A parent told a story about a gang incident involving one of his children; someone else talked about a woman whose son had committed suicide, and she was visiting the woman as a member of the church's lay pastoral care team; another asked if we only admit we need God in a crisis; someone else acknowledged the desire for revenge she had while going through her divorce. Actually hearing, *out loud*, the painful cries of this psalmist made an enormous difference in the depth of responses.

This group experience is certainly not an argument against reading the psalms privately and silently; we have already seen the transformative power of these psalms for private prayer in some of the individuals' stories in the introduction. What it does support is the importance of praying psalms of sorrow and suffering in *community*, as it has been important throughout the history of psalmody. Acknowledging feelings and experiences of disorientation in the act of corporate worship through praying, singing, and saying these psalms allows us to support one another in placing the experiences and emotions before God.

CHAPTER TWO

Remember Your Congregation
Psalms in Communal Prayer and Worship

You have made us like sheep for slaughter, and have scattered us among the
    nations.
All day long my disgrace is before me, and shame has covered my face
at the words of the taunters and revilers, at the slight of the enemy and the
    avenger.
All this had come upon us, yet we have not forgotten you, or been false to
    your covenant.
Our heart has not turned back, nor have our steps departed from your way,
yet you have broken us in the haunt of the jackals, and covered us with deep
    darkness. (Ps. 44:11, 15–19)

Hear my voice, O God, in my complaint; preserve my life from the dread
    enemy.
Hide me from the secret plots of the wicked, from the scheming of evildoers,
who whet their tongues like swords, who aim bitter words like arrows,
shooting from ambush at the blameless; they shoot suddenly and without fear.
But God will shoot his arrow at them; they will be wounded suddenly.
    (Ps. 64:1–4, 7)

When we pray and worship with our church congregations on Sundays,
we never experience an enormous body of spiritual material that has been
important to worshiping communities for more than twenty-five hundred
years. What are we missing, and why? These are the questions addressed in
this chapter, which begins by tracing the history of psalms in prayer and worship, then focuses on two psalms of lament that we never pray on Sundays,
and finishes with a discussion of some of the ways in which the psalms for
times of trouble might be more fully included in contemporary worship.

The book of Psalms represents the work of many poets and musicians
spanning the centuries from about 1200 to 500 B.C.E., and worshipers
passed the psalms down orally for many years before they were recorded
in written form. As lyric poetry, most psalms were intended to be sung or
chanted, some for special occasions and festivals. Described as the "hymn
book" of the Second Temple, which was rebuilt in 520–515 B.C.E. by
those returning from exile in Babylonia, the psalms were sung by choirs,

accompanied by rich orchestras. Psalm 150 names instruments for praising God in the sanctuary: trumpet, lute, harp, tambourine, strings, pipes, cymbals. Scholars believe that the Psalter was canonized about A.D. 90, although the psalms were probably adopted at a much earlier date (Shepherd 19–20, 28). The book of Psalms is a collection of many smaller psalm collections and likely incorporates only a selected portion of the many psalms that had been composed and sung. Divided into five books—Book 1 (1–41), Book 2 (42–72), Book 3 (73–89), Book 4 (90–106), and Book 5 (107–150)—each section ends with a doxology, and Psalm 150 serves as a doxology for the entire book of Psalms. This ordering is thought by scholars to suggest that the first three books are the oldest, and that the last two books came later but incorporated many psalms from earlier collections (Shepherd 21–22).

The psalms include hymns of praise, portions of liturgy, affirmations of faith, expressions of thanksgiving, statements of wisdom, and mixed songs, but the greatest number of psalms (about 40 percent) are those that address individual and community situations of difficulty, such as laments and penitential psalms, discussed in chapter 1 as psalms of disorientation. It is evident from the completed collection that the particular 150 psalms included in the book of Psalms for devotional and liturgical life are clearly intended to encompass sadness, trouble, terror, rage, and suffering, as well as joy, praise, thanksgiving, and hope.

As a vehicle for Christian prayer, the psalms came into widespread use through the daily devotions and services in monastic communities in both the East and the West during the fourth century. The psalms were the basic substance of the monastic vocation: a life of prayer. The Rule of St. Benedict, which became the foundation for religious orders in the West, distributed the psalms among eight daily offices so that all 150 psalms were sung during a week. In addition to the liturgical offices, monks' days were filled with private prayer, and it was not uncommon for a monk to recite the entire Psalter in a day, a discipline carried on by the early Celtic monks of Ireland (Shepherd 56–58, 66). In monastic practice, monks certainly didn't shy away from psalms that included references to "enemies." Enemies were considered to be all the things, such as sin, that hold us back from God. Nor did they shy away from sorrow and struggle. Merton writes in *Bread in the Wilderness* that in the psalms, we find a "suffering just as concrete as our own, and more profound." The desert fathers "did not simply 'consider' the Psalm as they passed over it, drawing from it some pious reflection, or twirling one of its verses between their fingers as a spiritual nosegay. . . . They allowed their sorrows to be swallowed up in the sorrows of this mysterious Personage and they found themselves swept away, on the strong tide of his hope, into the very depths of God" (92–93).

Unlike the lectionaries for Sunday worship, such as the *Revised Common Lectionary*, our Daily Office lectionaries retain the cycle of appointing all of the psalms over a fixed period. The Daily Office Lectionary of the Episcopal *Book of Common Prayer*, for example, arranges readings in a two-year cycle, with the psalms appointed in a seven-week cycle recurring throughout the year except for variations during Lent and Easter seasons. Some of the psalms have brackets or parentheses to indicate whole psalms [in brackets] and verses (in parentheses) that can be omitted. Psalms of disorientation including 58, 59, 60, 70, 120, and 127 have brackets. Among the psalms with verses in parentheses are Psalm 63 (vv. 9–11):

> May those who seek my life to destroy it go down into the depths of the earth;
> Let them fall upon the edge of the sword, and let them be food for jackals.
> But the king will rejoice in God; all those who swear by him will be glad;
> For the mouth of those who speak lies shall be stopped;

and Psalm 110 (vv. 6–7):

> He will heap high the corpses; he will smash heads over the wide earth.
> He will drink from the brook beside the road; therefore he will lift high his head. (*The Book of Common Prayer*)

Unless a person regularly prays/reads the Daily Office or attends daily Eucharist, the experience of psalms in worship occurs during a Sunday service. As a result, those psalms excluded from the Sunday Lectionary are never heard at all.

Psalms of Lament: What We Lose

Fewer than a quarter of the individual and communal laments in the book of Psalms are ever prayed in full by congregations that follow the lectionaries such as the *Revised Common Lectionary* discussed in chapter 1. According to the *Revised Common Lectionary*, the appointed psalm "is a congregational response and meditation on the first reading, and is not intended as another reading" (*Revised Common Lectionary* 11). In other words, the appointed psalm on Sunday is not intended to be an independent lesson like the Old Testament reading, New Testament reading, and the Gospel. In personal correspondence with Chris Haslam, author of *Commentaries on the Revised Common Lectionary*, and Alan T. Perry, reviewer for that publication, those making selections for the RCL apparently felt that the "Psalms of lament were inappropriate responses" to the first reading or, put in another way, "were not chosen as appropriate meditations on the readings. This dynamic is also the reason why there is no apparent effort to read through all the Psalms, either systematically or otherwise, in the three-year cycle" (Haslam).

Why aren't they "appropriate" meditations? Extremely bad things, described in gruesome detail, happen to people in the psalms. In just the two examples cited above for the omission of verses in the Daily Office, some people are sent down to the depths of the earth, some fall on the edge of the sword and are food for jackals, corpses are piled up, and heads are smashed over the wide earth. Psalm 137 ends with the harshest verse in the entire Psalter: "Happy shall they be who take your little ones and dash them against the rock!" (v. 9). The complainers in the psalms not only have enemies, they pray for the harshest of possible retributions against them, appealing to a God who gets angry and shows it. They complain of undeserved suffering. Many of the ways in which the psalmists attempt to get God to act are openly manipulative. Some of the psalms are just too long for efficient Sunday praying. Is there any reason we would *want* to sing about all of this in church? Let's look at two powerful psalms of lament that we never hear in church and see what we are missing.

Psalm 44 and Psalm 64 are two of the psalms never prayed in Sunday services by congregations using the *Revised Common Lectionary*. A "lament," whether individual (Psalm 64) or communal (Psalm 44), is a complaint: a cry to God for deliverance from some kind of trouble, problem, or distress. Although these expressions sound intensely personal, they were closely tied to temple liturgy, to recurrent acts of worship. What appears to be a spontaneous outpouring actually fits a stylized and traditional structure (Holladay 42). It would be interesting to know more detail about the content and practice of these liturgies and how the psalms fit into them. Holladay points out, however, that "Scholars have tried to gain clarity about these questions without much success." What we do know is that the psalms were sung or chanted, probably with musical accompaniment, and that the psalmists demonstrated remarkable poetic skill (46).

Although no two psalms are exactly alike in incorporating the common elements of a lament, some do not have all of them, and some go back and forth several times repeating the elements, the structure of a lament is characterized by two parts, the first a statement of the problem and need for God's help (the plea), and the second a statement of trust in God's response (praise). The plea includes (1) a personal, intimate address to God asking for help; (2) a description of the problem with enough detail to demonstrate the psalmist's desperation; (3) a specific list of what God needs to do to solve the problem; (4) motivations for God to act, such as the innocence of the psalmist or the guilt of the speaker who is in need of forgiveness, the recollection of God's deeds in the past, the psalmist's value to God (so should not be permitted to perish), and God's own power and reputation; and (5) sometimes the request for imprecations, the smashing and bashing against those causing the problems. The psalm then turns to praise, and things are dramatically different: "Something has changed. We cannot ever know whether it is a changed circumstance, or changed attitude, or something of both. But the speaker now speaks differently" (Brueggemann, *Message 56*). In this second part, there is (6) an assurance that God has heard the plea, and (7) a doxology, offering praises and thanksgivings to God, acknowledging God as generous and faithful.

The two parts are clearly delineated in Psalm 64:

Plea (vv. 1–6)
Address: O God (v. 1).

Description of problem: Secret plots of the wicked, scheming of evildoers who whet their tongues like swords and aim bitter words like arrows, shooting from ambush at the blameless, holding fast to their evil purpose, talking of laying snares, thinking out a cunningly deceived plot (vv. 2–6).

Actions Needed: Hear my voice, preserve my life from the dread enemy, hide me from the secret plots of the wicked (vv. 1–2).

Motivation for God to Act: (Innocence of the speaker) Shooting from ambush at the blameless (v. 4).

Imprecations: God will shoot his arrow at them; they will be wounded; God will bring them to ruin (vv. 7–8).

Praise (vv. 8–10)
Assurance of being heard: Those who see will shake and fear; they will tell what God has brought about and ponder what God has done (vv. 8–9).

Doxology: Let the righteous rejoice in the Lord and take refuge in him. Let all the upright in heart glory (v. 10).

For a Sunday worship service, there are all sorts of things wrong with this form of prayer. It is repetitive. The subject matter is unpleasant, with an emphasis on complaining about everything that's wrong. It encourages bargaining with God to get what we want. The imprecations certainly don't fit Jesus' teachings about treatment of others. But it is this very structure that generates the dramatic movement within the psalms of lament, from despair to hope, from anguish to trust in God, sometimes back and forth several times, not unlike the emotional swings we experience when we are suffering. People who are grieving, for example, go up and down, back and forth, in the process that eventually leads to reorganization and renewed energy for life, where there are still waves of grief but the waves no longer dominate. For those mired in distress, this dynamic process is what helps lead eventually to a place of new orientation. The lament's structure can also be helpful in preaching the psalms, discussed in a later section of the chapter. (Also see the discussion of parallelism in chapter 4 for a consideration of how the seeming repetitiveness of the psalms may contribute to movement).

We do not know the many authors of the 150 psalms in the book of Psalms or exactly when each was composed. Based on historical references, linguistic analysis, citations of the psalms in Scripture, and other scholarly approaches, however, we do have some idea about their origins. Scholars believe that both Psalm 44 and Psalm 64 originated before the exile that began in 587 B.C.E. when Jerusalem was captured by the Babylonians. Linguistic features and historical references in Psalm 44, for example, suggest that it came from the northern kingdom, which existed from 922 B.C.E. to 721 B.C.E. It is thought that this psalm, the communal lament of a nation that has suffered a humiliating defeat but has not forgotten God, was used in an autumn liturgy known as the Festival of Booths, the only festival recorded for the northern kingdom (Holladay 28, 29). In his Letter to the Romans, Paul quotes from Psalm 44 to illustrate the persecution faced by early Christians:

"Because of you we are being killed all day long, and accounted as sheep for the slaughter." (Ps. 44:22)
"For your sake we are being killed all day long; we are accounted as sheep to be slaughtered." (Rom. 8:36)

Psalm 64 is a turning to God for help in a crisis in which personal enemies attack through their words. It is an individual lament believed to be older than Jeremiah because it is among the 16 psalms cited by the prophet, who is thought to have lived in the years leading up to the exile. From the Dead Sea Scrolls we also know that this psalm was used in one of the thanksgiving hymns composed in the Qumran Community and discovered in the Scrolls, along with the text of most of the 150 psalms in the book of Psalms, as well as other noncanonical psalms (Holladay 41, 107, 108).

Even this brief sketch of the psalms' history shows that one thing we lose by not praying these psalms in Sunday worship is hearing some of the psalms that have been part of worship since the earliest documentation of psalms in worship and that were significant to later scriptural writings. This background provides a historical context for considering the current use of these psalms and their relevance to contemporary worshipers. Although the cultural and worshiping context is different for us from that of the periods when the psalms were composed, human nature is not. The psalms connect us to those who lived and worshiped many hundreds of years ago because, as Merton writes, "The Psalms bring our hearts and minds into the presence of the living God . . . and the Psalms are theology. That means that they place us in direct contact with God" (16, 18–19). Psalms 44 and 64 offer theological themes that are important to current worshipers, as the following two stories illustrate.

Psalm 44

Sometimes referred to as the Holocaust Prayer, Psalm 44 is used at annual Holocaust memorial gatherings in many parts of the world where Jews and persons of other faiths come together to honor the memory of those who died in the Holocaust. The psalm begins with a remembrance of and thanksgiving for God's deeds of old: "You with your own hand drove out the nations. . . . You have saved us from our foes. . . . In God we have boasted continually, and we will give thanks to your name forever" (vv. 2, 7–8). But the current situation is horrible: "You have rejected us and abased us. . . . All day long my disgrace is before me. . . . Because of you we are being killed all day long, and accounted as sheep for the slaughter" (9, 15, 22). It is a slaughter of the virtuous: "Our heart has not turned back, nor have our steps departed from your way" (v. 18). The psalm is a communal prayer to God made in a circumstance of intense suffering by the innocent, but who remain faithful to God from this place of deep darkness: "For we sink down to the dust; our bodies cling to the ground. Rise up, come to our help" (vv. 25–26).

David R. Blumenthal, professor of Judaic studies at Emory University, relayed in an e-mail communication what he described as a "VERY impressive" use of Psalm 44 in a Holocaust Day service that he attended on the university campus. One student read Psalm 44 in its entirety, and then repeated the psalm's accusatory verses:

> Yet you have rejected us and abased us, and have not gone out with our armies.
> You made us turn back from the foe, and our enemies have gotten spoil.
> You have made us like sheep for the slaughter, and have scattered us among the nations.
> You have sold your people for a trifle, demanding no high price for them. . . .
> Because of you we are being killed all day long, and accounted as sheep for the slaughter. (vv. 9–12, 22)

While those verses were being repeated, another student read a section from Elie Wiesel's *Night*:

> Never shall I forget that night, the first night in camp, which has turned my life into one long night, seven times cursed and seven times sealed. Never shall I forget that smoke. Never shall I forget the little faces of the children, whose bodies I saw turned into wreaths of smoke beneath a silent blue sky.
>
> Never shall I forget those flames which consumed my faith forever.
>
> Never shall I forget that nocturnal silence which deprived me, for all eternity, of the desire to live. Never shall I forget those moments which murdered my God and my soul and turned my dreams to dust. Never shall I forget these things, even if I am condemned to live as long as God Himself. Never. (32)

Then, the Wiesel reading moved to undertone, and the remaining psalm verses came back up in a normal reading voice (Blumenthal "Re: Query").

In his article, "Confronting the Character of God," Blumenthal writes that Psalm 44 is "one of the most angry moments in biblical literature, so angry that the rabbis repressed its liturgical recitation." In a class he was teaching, Blumenthal once asked a student to read Psalm 44, and after several attempts she understood that it needed to be read with more power. He suggested that she read it again, setting it in winter 1945 Auschwitz (just before the liberation). "The young woman, who later became a minister, prayed it so powerfully that I could not talk when she finished. . . . The act of praying this psalm in the context of the Holocaust is an act of 'embracing pain,' almost infinite pain." Regarding such scripture, Blumenthal believes that we cannot understand God or ourselves if we censor out the parts that we do not like (Blumenthal "Confronting" 5).

Psalm 64

Ruth, a hospital chaplain, leads the hospital's Sunday worship service once a month, and in a recent homily she preached on the psalms as a "conversation with God." She said that while some of the psalms are uplifting and comforting, many are about things in our lives that are not pleasant at all. Those were the ones that she wanted to discuss that day because they acknowledged the dark feelings that we all have. With her sweet demeanor, Ruth shocked the congregation by reading verses from psalms with themes of anger, abuse, guilt, alienation, and terror. Included in the examples were verses from Psalm 64 about those who use words as weapons, the "evildoers who whet their tongues like swords, shooting from ambush at the blameless" (vv. 2–4). Ruth works closely with patients in the hospital's psychology unit and is aware of their feelings of shame about being there, but also their distress about what others say about them, calling them names like "Psycho," "Weirdo," "Crazy-Dude," and "Drunk." She says that people in the congregation "really sat up and listened," some obviously appalled at her choice of Scripture, but many nodding in agreement, and thanking her afterwards. She finished with the idea that there is hope of resolution through these conversations with God, and prayed the last verses of Psalm 38: "Do not forsake me, O LORD, O my God, do not be far from me; make haste to help me, O LORD, my salvation" (vv. 21–22).

What we miss specifically by not praying Psalm 44 in corporate worship is the prayer of an innocent community experiencing disastrous and humiliating suffering, a community that turns to God but never turns its back on God. By not praying Psalm 64 in a Sunday service, we lose the opportunity to make communal pleas for God's intervention in situations of *verbal abuse*, a common occurrence for worshipers of Yahweh in 700

B.C.E. and a major cause of relationship and communication problems and failures in the twenty-first century C.E. A similar case could be made for other psalms of lament that do not appear in the Sunday lectionaries or that are used in an abbreviated form that changes their meaning.

The intent here, though, is not to argue for praying a psalm of disorientation every Sunday, but rather that our praying of the psalms should reflect the relative emphasis on these psalms and their themes in the book of Psalms and that our prayers generally should include lament. The text selections for the *Revised Common Lectionary* were finalized in 1993, and the RCL committee does not intend to revise them (Vanderbilt Divinity Library). Since for now the lectionary is not likely to change, we turn to some of the other ways in which these psalms might be incorporated into prayer and worship.

Preaching the Psalms

An eighty-six-year-old man in Ann's parish was brutally attacked in his home. On the following Sunday, while he was in the hospital in critical condition suffering from bullet and knife wounds, Ann preached a sermon about the incident. Wanting to acknowledge the anger and outrage that members of the congregation were feeling and at the same time move the congregation toward forgiveness, she preached the sermon using Psalm 58 as the text:

The wicked go astray from the womb; they err from their birth, speaking lies. . . .
O God, break the teeth in their mouths; tear out the fangs of the young lions,
    O Lord!
Let them vanish like water that runs away; like grass let them be trodden
    down and wither.
Let them be like the snail that dissolves into slime;
like the untimely birth that never sees the sun. . . .
People will say, "Surely there is a reward for the righteous;
surely there is a God who judges on earth." (vv. 3, 6–8, 11)

Recognizing its relevance to her congregation's worship on that difficult Sunday, Ann chose this psalm because it offered an invitation to cry out against the enemy, but to cry together within the context of prayer, within the embrace of a God who fully understands the evil that surrounds us and the condition of those who engage in it. She says that the idea of preaching on this psalm came from Gina Hens-Piazza, a professor at the Jesuit School of Theology, who had made the suggestion in a presentation on the psalms Ann had attended: "Keep the curse. It leads to catharsis which leads to confession which leads to communion." By basing her sermon on this psalm, Ann wanted the congregation to acknowledge and express their feelings, but to entrust the justice to God and to leave open the possibility that God could propel us towards forgiveness. People in the congregation found the sermon helpful, although one woman commented that "the path to forgiveness would be a very long path."

As this example shows, preaching the psalms is one way of incorporating psalms with themes of disorientation into Sunday worship to connect the experiences of the psalmists with our own, and we have excellent models of psalm-preaching by such notable preachers as Augustine, John Donne, Martin Luther, Dietrich Bonhoeffer, and Martin Luther King Jr. John Donne, for example, used Psalm 89:48, "What man is hee that liveth, and shall not see death?" as the text for his Easter sermon March 28, 1619, in which he also quotes from Psalm 90:10, "Mans age is seventy, and eighty is labour and pain." The sermon's theme, in which Donne answers the question that those who abide in Christ shall not see death, echoes his poem, "Death, be not proud": "One short sleep past, we wake eternally/And death shall be no more; Death, thou shalt die." Dietrich Bonhoeffer, who referred to the Psalter as 'The Prayer Book of the Bible," insisted that "one should not hurry by the passages of wrath and vengeance simply because they were jarring and bloody." His "Sermon on a Psalm of Vengeance" is based on Psalm 58, and in it he says, " It would mean much if we would learn that we must earnestly pray to God in such distress and that whoever entrusts revenge to God dismisses any thought of ever taking revenge himself" (4).

In spite of this rich history, the psalms are rarely preached in contemporary worship services. One reason is the function of the psalm in the service as a "gradual," meaning it is a response to the Old Testament reading in order to provide transition to the New Testament reading, with chanting by a cantor and refrain sung by the congregation or choir. Consequently, the psalm is not considered a standalone lesson in the way other Scriptures are, but a response to a reading. Other reasons the psalms are rarely preached, according to clergy I have consulted, include the preferred preaching focus on the Gospel, the general emphasis in Christian churches on the New Testament, and the psalms' many unsavory and grisly themes.

Old Testament professor J. Clinton McCann and Methodist pastor James C. Howell are two preachers who take exception to this list of reasons. Authors of *Preaching the Psalms*, they believe the psalms are meant to be preached. In addition to discussing the "why" of preaching the psalms—such as learning truths about ourselves and finding ways of bringing in prayer all conditions of human needs and hopes to God—the authors offer a helpful model of how to preach the psalms. They suggest that the psalms' great wealth of imaginative images, metaphors, and figures can provide a marvelous entry into sermons: a despised worm, a nesting stork, a war horse, packs of dogs, sheep grazing, wings, the dew, hail, flowers, a thundercloud, a stone fortress, a deer sniffing the air for water.

McCann and Howell encourage readers to turn their imaginations loose on these images: "Each is like a still life. We take our watches off, and then we examine the color, we weigh the density, we listen for the breeze, we follow the scent, we savor the wine's aftertaste" (51). Psalm 42 begins with the image of a deer longing for water, which is compared to the psalmist's thirst for God. The authors include in their book the text of an entire sermon on Psalm 42 (65–68).

The psalms are not static. They begin in one place, with a certain mood or situation, and then they move, transporting the psalmist and the reader to a new place, a new situation, an altered mood. Another McCann and Howell suggestion for preaching the psalms is to follow that inner dynamic of the psalm from where it begins to the place that it takes us (69). This approach of following the movement through the psalm can be used in preaching a sermon on almost any psalm, but it is especially appropriate to the laments, where the movement is dramatic—in part because of the lament's structure, which moves us from complaint and suffering to pleas for help, to expressions of trust and praise.

Consider Psalm 3, the first individual lament in the book of Psalms:

> O Lord, how many are my foes! Many are rising up against me; many are
> saying to me,
> "There is no help for you in God."
> But you, O Lord, are a shield around me, my glory, and the one who lifts up
> my head.
> I cry aloud to the Lord, and he answers me from his holy hill.
> I lie down and sleep; I wake again, for the Lord sustains me.
> I am not afraid of ten thousands of people who have set themselves against
> me all around.
> Rise up, O Lord! Deliver me, O my God!
> For you strike all my enemies on the cheek; you break the teeth of the wicked.
> Deliverance belongs to the Lord; may your blessing be on your people!

When we enter the psalm, the psalmist is among foes who are rising up and insisting that God cannot help, which taps deeply into the psalmist's vulnerability. The metaphors for God are "shield," "glory," and "the one who lifts my head," images of protection and nurture. If God cannot help, the situation seems truly dim. A preacher could then talk about the ways in which we hear that message in contemporary culture—from family and friends, at our workplace, in our social gatherings, at sporting events, through the media, possibly even at church—and how we respond to it. The movement, though, in Psalm 3 is to God, in spite of this message. The psalmist demonstrates belief that there is help in God, so ever-present that God enables our basic life rhythms: "I lie down and sleep; I wake again, for the Lord sustains me." Foes rise up, but so, too, does "my head" rise up because God lifts it. The desired vindication in the psalm, striking enemies on the cheek and breaking the teeth of the wicked, reflects the depth of the psalmist's pain. That's what we do when we are hurt—we lash out. Here, the psalmist is taking that desire for vengeance to God rather than acting on the feelings. The movement in the psalm continues toward deliverance and finishes with a blessing.

A related approach to preaching the psalms is to focus on the movement of an individual or community in response to the psalm. I have preached a sermon on Psalm 52, using the story of Georgia, the hospice patient in the book's introduction with whom I sang the vengeful verses, helping her vent her anger. In Psalm 52, it is God that expresses anger by wreaking havoc on those who love evil, those who trust in abundant riches and seek refuge in wealth. God breaks them down, snatches them from their tent, uproots them in the land of the living. Ultimately, I believe that through the expressing and healing of her anger, Georgia became like the "green olive tree in the house of God," trusting "in the steadfast love of God" (Ps. 52:8).

In the sermon on Psalm 58 that began this section, the preacher allowed the words of the psalm to express the community's feelings of anger, outrage, and injustice. By folding the psalm into the liturgy, however, she enabled the congregation to express the feeling as a prayer, enfolded by God's love, compassion, and understanding, with the intended movement toward forgiveness of the perpetrators. This sermon is an example of bringing a situation to the psalm, which is an idea similar to that described in the book's introduction, the sermon based on Psalm 37 that was preached in my church following the event of 9/11. Through the psalm, our perspective was transformed in a way that enlarged our vision and understanding of who is the "victim" and who is the "enemy."

McCann and Howell believe that preaching the psalms involves helping listeners understand that happiness is not *incompatible* with suffering. They point out that this is no easy task in a culture that systematically tries to teach us that suffering and pain are aberrations to be avoided or denied or defused by something we buy to make us feel better (McCann and Howell 105). It is no easy task in church, either, if we hear, through our liturgies, that suffering and pain are aberrations to be avoided or denied or defused.

Special Services and Church Programs

Another way in which the lament and penitential psalms can be more fully used is in special services, such as the Holocaust memorial service described in connection with Psalm 44. This does not further the objective of using these psalms in Sunday worship, but it would incorporate them more fully into communal worship generally. When my own parish had several members diagnosed with cancer in a short period of time, we held a prayer vigil for cancer patients from eight a.m. to eight p.m. on a weekday. Participants from other churches joined us, some signing up to be in the church for an hour or two, others stopping by the church as they could before and after work and during the day. Names were placed in a basket on the altar, candles were lit throughout the church, and kneeling stations were available. The vigil began and ended with the *Litany of Healing* from *The Book of Occasional Services 1994*. Lists of recommended psalms and other Scriptures were set out, including the following:

Psalm 13: "How long, O LORD? Will you forget me forever? How long will you hide your face from me? How long must I bear pain in my soul, and have sorrow in my heart all day long? How long shall my enemy be exalted over me?" (vv. 1–2)

Psalm 27: "When evildoers assail me to devour my flesh—my adversaries and foes—they shall stumble and fall." (v. 2)

Psalm 91: "You will not fear the terror of the night, or the arrow that flies by day, or the pestilence that stalks in darkness, or the destruction that wastes at noonday." (vv. 5–6)

Psalm 130: "Out of the depths I cry to you, O LORD. LORD, hear my voice! Let your ears be attentive to the voice of my supplications! My soul waits for the Lord more than those who watch for the morning, more than those who watch for the morning." (vv. 1–2, 6)

This vigil format with psalms and other appropriate Scriptures could be used for many other circumstances, such as for those suffering from other kinds of diseases, as well as for conditions in the world such as war and social injustices. My parish participates in a countywide domestic violence awareness vigil and candlelight walk, and we are considering holding future vigils in connection with other community activities, such as peace marches and walks for AIDS, Alzheimer's disease, breast cancer, heart disease, and diabetes.

Another program at my parish was an Advent series on the psalms, meeting Wednesday evenings with a soup and bread supper, followed by a presentation and discussion. One of the week's sessions focused specifically on the psalms of disorientation. The series concluded with each participant composing a psalm, and some wrote laments.

One large Methodist church, Davidson United Methodist Church in Davidson, North Carolina, experimented with an all-encompassing approach to the psalms by focusing its worship and spiritual life on the psalms for an entire church season, the season after Pentecost, from May through August. This process involved planning and cooperation from the church staff as well as the lay congregational leaders. The senior pastor preached a series of sermons on the psalms; the minister of music selected anthems and other music on the psalms; the congregation participated in workshops covering basic teachings about the psalms; Sunday school classes and other small groups used a video-based curriculum on the psalms; and the entire congregation was asked to pray the psalms, with a calendar of selections designed to be in sync with the psalms that would be read and preached on Sundays. Each Sunday's bulletin had an insert on that week's psalms with historical background and insights related to musical aspects of the psalm. Surveys of the congregation indicated that people did read and pray the psalms, many for the first time in their lives, and they discussed the psalms in living rooms, classrooms, and restaurants—extending the series well beyond the worship services (Howell 123–142). This psalms immersion idea could be adapted in various ways of time and content to fit a church's rhythms and activities.

A final idea I would like to suggest is to hold a service of lament that is based on the form of lament psalms. Study of the lament psalms has shown their enormous theological significance in the faith and liturgy of Israel as well as in their subsequent use by the church. If worship is to reflect the range of human experience as well as the condition of the world, lament is an essential component. A service based on the lament structure could have an order such as the following:

Plea

Part 1

Opening prayer and psalms

—A prayer addressing God intimately, such as: "O God of peace, who has taught us that in returning and rest we shall be saved, in quietness and in confidence shall be our strength: By the breath of your Spirit, fill us with your presence, that we may be still and know that you are God; through Jesus Christ our Lord. Amen." Following the prayer, participants might be asked to say silently or aloud the name or names they use when they address God in prayer.

—Responsorial reading or chanting of an individual lament (e.g., Ps. 13 or 25 or 70) and a communal lament (e.g., Ps. 74 or 80 or 126).

Part 2

The expression of pleas to God, with congregants naming silently or aloud their specific requests. Those who make their pleas out loud should be encouraged to do so in whatever tone of voice they would like to use—e.g., shouting or crying out or groaning. At the conclusion, the leader says, "We pray," and all say, "O God, hear our prayers."

Part 3

Prayers for God's response to the needs expressed, silently or aloud, naming the actions desired in relation to the prayer requests, again using whatever tone the congregants choose. At the conclusion, the leader says, "We pray," and all say, "O God, hear our prayers."

Part 4

Motivations for God to Act
1 Chronicles 16:7–34

Part 5

Confession, Absolution, Peace

Praise and Thanksgiving

Part 6

Assurance of Being Heard
Gospel: Luke 17:11–19
The celebration of Holy Eucharist using a Eucharistic Prayer for Communal Lament (see below) that encompasses communal lament for the state of the world, the state of the environment, the state of the church, and the human condition, in the context of God's actions through history to relieve human suffering, anguish, disharmony, and alienation.
The Lord's Prayer
Communion of the People

Part 7

Prayer of thanksgiving
Sing the "Doxology"
Dismissal Blessing

Eucharistic Prayer for Communal Lament

God be with you
And also with you.
Lift up your hearts.
We lift them to our God.
Let us thank our loving God.
To God we offer thanks and praise.

It is good and right to praise you, O God, source of light and life, and to give you thanks for the gifts of creation. The heavens are the work of your hands. The earth is yours, and all that is in it. Yours is the day, but yours also is the night, and when we are in darkness, you are merciful and life-giving. Therefore we acclaim you, joining our voices with all your creation to sing this hymn of praise:

Holy, holy, holy is the God of hosts.
The whole earth is full of your glory.
Blessed is the one who comes in the name of our God.
Hosanna in the highest.

We glorify you, O God, for your creation and for the covenant which you gave to your people. When your people suffered and expressed anguish, you offered liberation, comfort, and hope. And when your people were again overwhelmed by disharmony and alienation, you sent your only son, Jesus Christ, to share in their sufferings and to make a unique offering of redemption through his life, death, resurrection, and ascension.

When the hour came, Jesus took his place at the table, his disciples with him. He took bread and after blessing it broke it, gave it to the disciples and said, "Take, eat; this is my body. Do this for the remembrance of me." Then he took a cup of wine and after giving thanks, he gave it to them, saying, "Drink from it all of you, for this is the blood of the covenant, which is poured out for many for the forgiveness of sins. Do this, as often as you drink it, in remembrance of me."

As we celebrate and share in this sacred meal, we remember Christ's sacrifice, offering our thanksgiving for Christ's death, resurrection, and ascension.

Christ is with us, and we are in Christ.

Send your Holy Spirit to sanctify these holy gifts of food and drink to be the body and blood of Christ in your new covenant. Unite us as one body to be the bearers of this covenant in the world, reflecting your eternal light, while acknowledging the constant need for your redeeming love.

Where there is violence, oppression, hunger, and poverty,

We lament the condition of the world. Guide us in the ways of justice, peace, and compassion.

Where there is disaster, carelessness, selfishness, and misuse of the environment,

We lament the condition of the earth. Help us be responsible stewards of your creation.

Where the church is unable or unwilling to minister,

We lament the condition of the church. Show us how to serve all your people.

Where there is sickness, suffering, grief, abuse, addiction, brokenness, and sorrow,

We lament the human condition. Fill us with your grace.

In the communion of the saints, we lament as faithful witnesses to the resurrection of Jesus Christ. Accept these our prayers, O God, through Jesus Christ, and in the unity of the Holy Spirit. Amen. *

*Lyn M. Fraser, Episcopal Theological Seminary of the Southwest, December 2002

When we worship on Sundays, we never pray many of the psalms that were composed to ask for God's help in our communal and individual experiences of anguish, alienation, and grief. As a result we do not express communally what we are feeling during these times. Lectionary planners have taken a different approach to the psalms than did the editors of the book of Psalms, who apparently believed that we should pray much more frequently about our difficulties. This chapter has presented some of the ways in which we might do that though preaching on the psalms; through using the psalms as a resource in special services and vigils; through a broad-ranging congregational program that puts psalms at the center of sermons, music, prayer, and study; and by holding a service of lament that is based on the structure of lament psalms. Another way to hear the laments would be to use those psalms in full when they are assigned in the lectionary rather than eliminating verses that readers find unpleasant. David N. Power, O.M.I., is the professor of systematic theology and liturgy at Catholic University of America and author of A *Eucharist in an Age of Abandonment*. He suggests, in his article "The Eucharistic Prayer: Another Look," that disorientation cannot be suffered without lament, and the Eucharistic memorial has to be renewed through lament: "To give thanks, the community must weep, and the two may be strangely combined" (251). For more than twenty-five hundred years, the psalmists have provided us with a ready vocabulary of appropriate prayer.

శ

PART TWO

Pastoral Care

శ

じ

CHAPTER THREE

My Heart Is Stricken

Ministering to the Terminally Ill and Bereaved

Yea, though I walk through the valley of the shadow of death, I will fear no evil:
for thou art with me; thy rod and thy staff they comfort me.
Thou preparest a table before me in the presence of mine enemies:
thou anointest my head with oil; my cup runneth over.
Surely goodness and mercy shall follow me all the days of my life:
and I will dwell in the house of the Lord for ever. (Ps. 23:4–6, KJV)

I will lift up mine eyes unto the hills, from whence cometh my help.
My help cometh from the Lord, which made heaven and earth. . . .
The LORD shall preserve thee from all evil: he shall preserve thy soul.
The LORD shall preserve thy going out and thy coming in
from this time forth, and even for evermore. (Ps. 121:1–2, 7–8, KJV)

In her pioneering work *On Death and Dying,* Elisabeth Kubler-Ross made a significant contribution to our society's understanding of the dying process and, perhaps even more importantly, to our willingness to talk about death and dying. Writing out of her clinical experience with terminally ill patients while teaching psychiatry at the University of Chicago, she observed five stages her patients experienced in the process of dying: denial, bargaining, anger, depression, and acceptance. In the years since the book's publication in 1969 the Kubler-Ross model, with modifications, has been widely used by those who work with terminally ill patients and has also been adapted to other situations, such as bereavement. Regardless of one's affinity with the order and number of Kubler-Ross's stages, the issues she addresses are important to all who work with the terminally ill as well as with their caregivers and with those who are bereaved.

One of the major insights that Kubler-Ross documented in her work with the terminally ill is how much we can learn from those who are dying, and not just about dying but about living, faith, hope, compassion, and the healing that is possible when there is no cure. In the process of writing this book, I have had conversations and communication with numerous pastoral caregivers—clergy, hospital chaplains, hospice spiritual care staff— from around the country in a variety of health-care environments. Based on these interviews, the most widely used psalm in work with the terminally ill, by an overwhelming margin, is the King James Version of Psalm 23, with Psalm 121 following a distant second. (Both psalms are cited at the beginning of the chapter.) Another widely used psalm is Psalm 139 with its image of God's spirit with us no matter where we are, even in the dark, which to God is the same as light:

> Where can I go from your spirit? Or where can I flee from your presence?
> If I ascend to heaven, you are there; if I make my bed in Sheol, you are there.
> If I take the wings of the morning and settle at the farthest limits of the sea,
> even there your hand shall lead me, and your right hand shall hold me fast.
> If I say, "Surely the darkness shall cover me, and the light around me become
>   night,"
> even the darkness is not dark to you; the night is as bright as the day,
> for darkness is as light to you. (vv. 7–12)

People who are dying or who are suffering from the death of a loved one want to hear something familiar and comforting. I agree with their choices, and I pray these psalms in my own work as well as well as privately. But what I have learned from the dying and in reports from other pastoral caregivers is that there are situations in which psalms of disorientation provide a unique spiritual witness; these psalms are the focus of this chapter.

Psalms and the Terminally Ill

In a general sense, the psalms are often helpful in settings such as hospice work that encompass a wide religious and nonreligious spectrum among patients and family members. We learn early on in hospice training and practical experience to separate "spiritual" from "religious" and "religious denomination" except insofar as they are intertwined for the patient. What matters is not whether a patient is Methodist or Greek Orthodox or Buddhist, but what is sacred for a patient or family member. That might mean Jesus Christ as personal savior, but it might also mean an array of backyard bird feeders. One of my hospice patients, Margaret, helped found a church in our area, a church that was visible from her living room window. While her Christian faith was obviously important to her, the time together that felt most spiritual was an entire afternoon we spent going through Margaret's collection of fishing lures, prompted by her desire to help me get "started right" on my own Colorado fishing. There were four full cases, and each lure held memories and a story—where it was used, what it caught or didn't, and who was with Margaret while she was fishing. She held each lure up to the light, turning it slowly in her hand as she talked about it. Hospice workers never enter a patient situation with religious or spiritual assumptions, but rather with an attitude of compassion and acceptance, open to the patient's own richly varied life.

As part of the hospice spiritual care team, my work is largely a ministry of presence: to listen and to affirm, to invite emotional expression and spiritual exploration. I find the psalms are helpful in exploring spiritual issues, regardless of the patient's religious or nonreligious framework. One of my patients, Dan, is an evangelical Christian who reads daily from a meditation guide that begins with a quotation from Scripture, often from a psalm. When I visit we read the guide together, and conversation is about the psalmist's theology in relation to Dan's own beliefs. At the other end of the spectrum, Kenneth is antireligion. Having left the Catholic Church in his thirties, he has no interest in religion in any form. When I visit, he shows me photos from his life as an artist on the West Coast, and we look through books that he values. Kenneth says that photographs and books are the things that most give meaning to his life because he can return to them again and again. He likes poetry and appreciates the psalms as classic literature, responding to their rhythms and vivid imagery. For each of these patients the psalms offer an opening to discussing spiritual issues and questions.

In providing a ministry of presence, pastoral caregivers to the terminally ill also help patients accomplish specific tasks, such as accepting the reality of imminent death, resolving issues of forgiveness and reconciliation, and expressing emotions associated with the dying process. There are specific psalms and portions of psalms that may be useful in assisting patients with the peaceful completion of this process. Psalm 71, a personal lament, is one example. The psalmist clearly acknowledges the need for a power greater than other people can provide at a time when our life's strength has been spent: "In you, O LORD, I take refuge. . . . Do not cast me off in the time of old age; do not forsake me when my strength is spent" (vv. 1, 9). It is clear from verse 4 that all is not pleasant in this psalmist's world: "Rescue me, O my God, from the hand of the wicked, from the grasp of the unjust and cruel" (v. 4). The psalmist has work to do in regard to others and carries strong emotions of hurt and anger associated with these relationships: "Let my accusers be put to shame and consumed; let those who seek to hurt me be covered with scorn and disgrace" (v. 13). But the psalmist expresses faith in God in dealing with these challenges: "You who have made me see many troubles and calamities will revive me again; from the depths of the earth you will bring me up again" (v. 20). Any one or all of these themes might be helpful in a hospice situation: recognizing the need for a power greater than ourselves, admitting that there are problems and praying for God's help in addressing them, conveying strong emotions resulting from past hurts, and recognizing God's reviving presence in the past and crying out for that in the present situation.

Psalm 71 was important in the dying process of Raymond, a man who was diagnosed with lung cancer in his early fifties. Raymond had complex issues from his past stemming from having been sexually abused; he had considerable difficulty expressing any emotions at all. Completely bald, he would comb through imaginary hair with his fingers rather than express his feelings. The hospice chaplain who visited Raymond said that initially he had no affect at all when he talked about his life, just stating his life history as a flat narrative. For use in prayer, the chaplain recommended to Raymond many psalms that expressed emotions about enemies, and that he should consider not only human enemies but also his cancer as his enemy. The chaplain told Raymond he could pray those psalms as a way of expressing things he had not been able to put into words. In addition to Psalm 71, Raymond used Psalm 13:

> How long, O Lord? Will you forget me forever? How long will you hide your face from me?
> How long must I bear pain in my soul, and have sorrow in my heart all day long?
> How long shall my enemy be exalted over me?
> My foes will rejoice because I am shaken.
> But I trusted in your steadfast love; my heart shall rejoice in your salvation.
> (vv. 1–2, 4–5)

and Psalm 55:

> Attend to me, and answer me; I am troubled in my complaint.
> I am distraught by the noise of the enemy, because of the clamor of the wicked.
> For they bring trouble upon me, and in anger they cherish enmity against me.
> My heart is in anguish within me, the terrors of death have fallen upon me.
> Fear and trembling come upon me, and horror overwhelms me. (vv. 55:2–5)

Raymond had difficulty accepting his terminal diagnosis in part because of his inability to express feelings: if he admitted he was going to die, then he might also have to express some rage and sadness. By using the psalms that prayed for revenge against enemies, including his cancer, he was able to begin venting his anger and other emotions. He had never said out loud how he felt, and the psalms gave him a way to do that. *Forgotten and abandoned. Sorrowful. Troubled. Distraught. Angry and anguished. Terrorized by death. Fearful.* Gradually, as he learned to be more open and expressive about his own feelings, he was able to be open to those of others, leading to forgiveness of those who had hurt him and of himself. In this process he achieved reconciliation with his ex-wife and with a son who had been estranged.

Forgiveness was also an important issue for Bernice, a terminal patient at the Veterans Administration hospital where I served as a chaplain intern. Bernice called me in one morning; always immaculately groomed, she had the top half of her hospital bed elevated and was sitting straight up as if she were chairing a meeting. Bernice announced decisively, "I want to make a confession." She didn't want a priest to come or to use a liturgy.

Looking through the copy of her Bible in the room, I suggested Psalm 51, and she agreed. Together, we read:

> Have mercy on me, O God, according to your steadfast love; according to your abundant mercy blot out my offenses.
> Wash me thoroughly from my iniquity, and cleanse me from my sin.
> For I know my transgressions, and my sin is ever before me. . . .
> Create in me a clean heart, O God, and put a new and right spirit within me.
> Do not cast me away from your presence, and do not take your holy spirit from me.
> Restore me to the joy of your salvation, and sustain me with a willing spirit.
> (vv. 1–3, 10–12)

She asked if God forgives our sins, even the "X-rated" ones. I assured her that God did, fully, both hers and mine. Bernice then told me she'd done a number of things as a young nurse during World War II that she regretted. She felt ashamed of what she had done. I asked her if she wanted to talk about these things, and she never said specifically what they were, but my impression was that they involved multiple sexual relationships. We talked about the need for God's forgiveness for things we have done as well as things we have left undone. She asked that we read the psalm again, which we did. Afterwards, Bernice said that she still regretted and was embarrassed by what she had done, but she felt forgiven by God.

Mortality

Accepting the fact that we will not live forever is essential to the terminally ill patient, but it is also necessary for a pastoral caregiver. The session from my own hospice training fifteen years ago that I remember most vividly is the evening during which a psychologist guided us through a meditation on our own deaths: from the diagnosis of terminal illness through our dying, a funeral or memorial service, and whatever we believed or did not believe came after that. In bereavement work also, one of the comments I hear over and over is that the death of a loved one has caused the bereaved to face for the first time her or his own fragility.

Of the Kubler-Ross stages, the one that the psalms do not speak to is denial. Instead, psalmists face mortality with a head-on leap into the reality of our life's end. In Psalm 39, the speaker asks of God, "LORD, let me know my end, and what is the measure of my days; let me know how fleeting my life is. You have made my days a few handbreadths, and my lifetime is as nothing in your sight" (vv. 4–5). Honestly acknowledging feelings of darkness associated with mortality, the psalm finishes with the request that God turn away: "Turn your gaze away from me, that I may smile again, before I depart and am no more" (v. 12). The psalmist is depressed, as reflected in the verse, "Remove your stroke from me; I am worn down by the blows of your hand" (v. 10). Along with the plunge into reality, however, is an awareness in the psalm's center of not jumping in alone: "And now, O Lord, what do I wait for? My hope is in you" (v. 39:7).

Spiritual caregivers who have used such psalms say that patients respond to the psalmists' sense of reality. Somewhat paradoxically, the full acceptance of death seems to release something that helps patients make a turn—not exactly to optimism but toward a sense of grace about the time that is left. One of the goals of hospice is to enhance the quality of life that remains for a patient, and this turn is an essential element in accomplishing that goal.

The fleetingness of life is also a subject of Psalm 90:

> You turn us back to dust, and say, "Turn back, you mortals."
> For a thousand years in your sight are like yesterday when it is past, or like a watch in the night.
> For all our days pass away under your wrath; our years come to an end like a sigh.
> The days of our life are seventy years, or perhaps eighty, if we are strong;
> even then their span is only toil and trouble; they are soon gone, and we fly away. (vv. 90:3–4; 9–10)

In this psalm, the prayer moves forward, not dwelling on the end of life but rather on what we do with the days that we have:

> So teach us to count our days that we may gain a wise heart.
> Satisfy us in the morning with your steadfast love, so that we may rejoice and be glad all our days.
> Let the favor of the Lord our God be upon us, and prosper the work of our hands—
> O prosper the work of our hands! (vv. 12, 14, 17)

Terminally ill patients are losing control of seemingly everything, and this psalm helps move the focus onto what they can still do "to prosper the work of our hands." One way of doing this is to leave something behind for those they love. As part of my own hospice work, I am involved with a program in which teen volunteers help patients record their life stories as a legacy for friends and family. This is an innovative way for patients to feel that they have complete control over something in their lives as well as to be able to create something tangible that benefits those they love.

Healing without Cure

When asked to explain the hospice philosophy of "healing without cure," the best way I know to do that is through the example of patients, such as Georgia, in the introduction to the book; or Raymond's story above; or Mary Louise, who experienced restoration of wholeness and soundness even though her illness was terminal. Mary Louise entered hospice after physicians prepared her and her family for an imminent death, within two or three months. As with many patients, she seemed more concerned about how she would die than with dying itself. In the midst of a casual discussion about ordinary things, like whether to use walnuts or pecans in making brownies, Mary Louise would slip in a comment that reflected her anxiety. In denial, the family was not supportive of her efforts to find out any more about how she would die. The hospice staff arranged for a nurse who specialized in Mary Louise's rare blood disease to come in for a conference. Mary Louise asked her questions, and the nurse responded openly, directly, and candidly. She explained the dying process for patients with the disease, some unpleasant possibilities, and what hospice could do to provide comfort. No other family member said a word during the meeting with the nurse, but when she left, the mood in the household had clearly changed. Mary Louise's anxiety was noticeably relieved by knowing the possible scenarios and what could be done about them. From that point on, the family could engage in discussions about her illness. Out-of-town family members came to say good-bye, then came back again several weeks later. The family celebrated family birthdays, Easter, and the Fourth of July. One morning before breakfast, Mary Louise fell asleep in her chair in the living room. Her husband called hospice. A nurse came, and they moved her back to the bed he and Mary Louise had shared every night for just a month shy of fifty years. Family members gathered around her bedside and kept watch. Shortly before midnight, Mary Louise died a peaceful death, her family with her. *This* is "healing without cure."

One of the psalms that conveys an understanding of healing without cure is Psalm 102. This psalm encompasses the recognition of death to come: "For my days pass away like smoke" (v. 3); an attempted bargaining with God to be allowed not to die: "'Oh my God,'" I say, "'do not take me away at the mid-point of my life'" (v. 24); and feelings of acute loneliness and despair, "I am like an owl of the wilderness, like a little owl of the waste places" (v. 6). Offering no promise of continued life, this psalm gracefully addresses the hospice hope of healing where there is no cure. But it ends on a note of reassurance with an awareness that the generations to follow will live securely because of the enduring presence of God: "But you are the same, and your years have no end. The children of your servants shall live secure; their offspring shall be established in your presence" (vv. 27–28).

As Ellen F. Davis writes, something does happen in Psalm 102, even though it is not the thing hoped for, which is not to be taken "away at the mid-point of my life. . . ." (v. 24). The change that occurs is a change that results from the act of praying:

> For the LORD will build up Zion . . . ; [God] will regard the prayer of the
> destitute, and will not despise their prayer.
> Let this be recorded for a generation to come, so that a people yet unborn
> may praise the Lord: that [God] looked down from his holy height . . .
> to set free those who were doomed to die. (vv. 16, 17, 18, 19, 20)

Davis says, "In a word, the change that takes place here is that our psalmist gains stability. The one who was on the brink of annihilation, discarded by God, who felt insubstantial as smoke, shadow, dried-up grass—now finds a voice, a standing place in the presence of God whose years are forever" (163).

The key to such movement forward in a hospice situation is not the kind of change in which the patient's health improves; it is a change in the person's attitude and emotions about ongoing physical deterioration and eventual death, and the trauma that surrounds that process. The prayer in Psalm 102 is a catalyst for the psalmist's personal transformation.

Raymond learned to express his emotions, to open up to others, to achieve reconciliation with family members, and to forgive. Knowledge about death from her disease relieved Mary Louise's anxiety, allowing her to live and to shake her family members out of their state of denial. Although this is not always the result, in Mary Louise's situation her life was not only enhanced in quality, but extended by many months. Georgia, the hospice patient whose story began this book, was able to express her raging fury at God through the psalms. She discovered that God gets mad, and the psalmists rage at God, so it must be all right for her, too. And they don't stay angry forever. The expression of that rich emotion and the change in her attitude helped Georgia move on to necessary decisions that enabled her to die a peaceful death.

Bereavement

Mending Hearts is a bereavement support group that I cofacilitate for my area hospice as part of a collaborative program with ten area churches. The group is open to adults who have experienced the death of a loved one and meets once a week throughout the year. We begin each session with an educational component, following a thirteen-week curriculum, and then open the session for general discussion. One of the topics we cover in the cycle is "Faith and Grieving," and I have regularly used psalms that explore grieving as part of that discussion.

The grieving process parallels the movement Brueggemann describes as the basis for his organization of psalms discussed in chapter 1. The common response to major loss is movement from relative stability into a period of severe disorientation, characterized by symptoms that may include numbness, depression, loss of appetite, sleeplessness, anger, guilt, fear, withdrawal, poor concentration, and physical pain. Working through the grieving process leads eventually to new orientation, when we are able to restore balance to our lives and reinvest our energies in productive ways. In a sense, grieving never ends because we continue to miss those we have lost, but we are able eventually to arrive at a place where the grief no longer dominates our lives. How this movement occurs and how long it takes varies considerably with each of us, depending on the circumstances and depth of the loss. It is not a straightforward process, but rather involves considerable back-and-forth, up-and-down movement, and the person who emerges is different, changed by the grieving process.

Through the Mending Hearts sessions, we attempt to provide a safe and supportive environment for people to accomplish the tasks of grieving. These tasks include (1) accepting the reality of the loss, (2) expressing the feelings associated with grief, (3) adjusting to an environment in which the deceased person is no longer present, and (4) reinvesting energy into what is in essence a new life.

As part of the discussion of "Faith and Grieving," the handout that I use presents excerpts from nine psalms, with the first column showing expressions of grief, and the second expressions of faith. The psalms themselves embody the journey through grief, as the psalmists move back and forth between anguish and hope, despair and trust, ultimately transforming sorrow into the sounds of joyful new song.

The Psalms and Grieving

GRIEF	FAITH
Psalm 6:6–7 I am weary with my moaning; every night I flood my bed with tears; I drench my couch with my weeping.	*Psalm 6:8–9* The Lord has heard the sound of my weeping. My eyes waste away because of grief. The Lord has heard my supplication; the Lord accepts my prayer.
Psalm 13:2 How long must I bear pain in my soul, and have sorrow in my heart all day long?	*Psalm 13:5–6* My heart shall rejoice in your salvation. I will sing because the Lord has dealt bountifully with me.
Psalm 31:9, 11 I am in distress; my eye wastes away from grief, my soul and body also. I am the scorn of all my adversaries, a horror to my neighbors, and object of dread to my acquaintances; those who see me in the street flee from me.	*Psalm 31:21–22* Blessed be the Lord, for the Lord has wondrously shown steadfast love to me when I was beset as a city under siege. You heard my supplication when I cried out for help.
Psalm 42:5 Why are you cast down, O my soul, and why are you so disquieted within me?	*Psalm 42:11* Hope in God; for I shall again praise [God], my help and my God.

Psalm 56:8
You have kept count of my tossings; put my tears In your bottle. Are they not in your record?

Psalm 56:12–13
I will render thank offerings to you. For you have delivered my soul from death, and my feet from falling, so that I may walk before God in the light of life.

Psalm 69:2–3
I sink in deep mire where there is no foothold; I have come into deep waters, and the flood sweeps over me. I am weary with my crying, and my throat is parched.

Psalm 69:30, 33
I will praise the name of God with a song. For the Lord hears the needy.

Psalm 77:2, 4–6
My soul refuses to be comforted. I am so troubled that I cannot speak. I consider the days of old, and remember the years of long ago. I commune with my heart in the night; I meditate and search my spirit.

Psalm 77:10, 13–14
And I say, "It is my grief that the right hand of the Most High has changed." Your way, O God, is holy. You are the God who works wonder.

Psalm 102: 4, 7
My heart is stricken and withered like grass; I am too wasted to eat my bread. I lie awake; I am like a lonely bird on the housetop.

Psalm 102:13, 17
You will rise up and have compassion. God will regard the prayer of the destitute.

Psalm 143:4, 7
My spirit faints within me; my heart within me is appalled. My spirit fails.

Psalm 143:9–10
I have fled to you for refuge. Let your good spirit lead me on a level path.

We begin by reading aloud the excerpts from the first column, and I ask for participants' responses. Although the discussion varies from group to group, the comments made at the most recent session as we went around the table reflect common responses. Marie and Janelle, both in their late seventies, have lost spouses to whom they had been married for more than fifty years. Marie refers to a verse from Psalm 77 about communing in the night and searching. She says she can get through her days pretty well, but everything hits in the night. She wakes up and cannot go back to sleep. Janelle agrees and says she stays awake and worries. Each says she slept only a couple of hours the night before.

Charles's wife died three months ago of congestive heart failure. He wears his white hair in a flattop because that's how he wore it when they met. Charles relates to the comment in Psalm 31 about being an object of "dread" to his acquaintances. When he was in the grocery store the day before, one of his friends on the bread aisle turned away from him. He worries that people don't want to see him because he's talked too much already about his wife's death. Frances, whose teenage son was killed in an automobile accident, nods, saying she only goes to the grocery store very early in the morning so she won't run into people she knows. It's especially hard if she sees someone who doesn't know of her son's death, and she has to tell them about his dying.

Rosa, who is grieving the death of her mother and a favorite uncle, likes the idea that God keeps our tears in a bottle. Several participants say it's easy to fill up a bottle. They do it all the time: the tears just flow, sometimes at unexpected times. We talk some about the tears of grieving as a source of healing, and that's why we always have plenty of tissue on the table at our meetings.

Jay's wife died at the age of forty-two from breast cancer. He relates to Psalm 143's failing spirit, and says that he feels like he is walking around in a "blanket of grief." Others nod.

Elsa, who is grieving the death of her husband from lung cancer and always knits during our sessions, responds to the "How long?" question in Psalm 13. She feels guilty about self-pity and not being able to get on with her life. We spend some time talking about the time period for grieving being an individual process, and that no one can know what that is for anyone else.

Noreen says that if she didn't know these quotations were from the psalms, she would think it was a transcript from a grief support group meeting. Everyone laughs.

Frances puts her head down on the table, then raises it and says, "What if we're not sure about our faith anymore? I've always gone to church, but now I'm just mad at God. Why did God take my son? He was a good person, he was going to be a doctor, he didn't drink or do drugs or sin. Look at all the other people around that God could have taken. Why my son?" The cofacilitator asks how that feels, to be angry at God. Frances says she's had fights with God before, and "God always wins." I'm not sure what she means, but she smiles when she says it, as if she still believes she and God are on the same team. We talk generally about the importance of expressing our feelings, that the group is a safe place to do that, and anger is a big part of grieving. Elsa says she thinks sometimes we're mad at God, but we shift the blame to someone else, a doctor or a family member. Janelle says we get mad at whoever's closest, but we're really just mad because we've lost the person we love.

Charles refers to the loss of appetite in Psalm 102 and talks about how hard it is to eat alone. Several others who have lost spouses affirm that difficulty.

I then introduce the second column of the handout, explaining that the psalmists don't just express the feelings and experiences of grief, but during a period of intense suffering they try to move out of that place by turning to a higher power, which for the psalmists is God. We read the excerpts from the second column.

Elsa immediately comments on the tone, that the first ones were "down," and these are more "up," more optimistic. Several people say that pretty much says it all, that's what their life is right now: up, down, up, down, and Elsa moves her hand like a roller coaster.

Jay says that the psalmists' trust in God reminds him of the Prayer of St. Francis of Assisi that his wife had on her bedside table, which he believes is about the potential for grace in life and he guesses in death as well. Noreeen feels like these prayers in the psalms are an "osmosis experience," unconsciously pervading our entire beings with some sort of spiritual fluid.

(I tell my cofacilitator after the meeting that Noreen and Jay should probably be writing this book.)

We finish with a general discussion of how the psalms might be helpful in grieving. One recurring comment from participants over several sessions is that the psalmists are honest in their descriptions of how awful they feel in grief, whatever its cause. Some members of the group find comfort in the expression that God is with us in these dark times, or, as the psalmist says, "Blessed be the Lord, for the Lord has wondrously shown steadfast love to me when I was beset as a city under siege" (Ps. 31:21). Another benefit of the psalms, according to people from the Mending Hearts group who have continued using them as a private resource, is that they help move us out of isolation, the feeling that we are all alone in our grief.

Although the discussion about grief presented here is within the context of one group's experience, the issues that come up—as psalms written more than two thousand years ago show—are universal. With the psalmists, we can release emotions, admit to bad days, question our faith, lose sleep, sob, tell our story over and over again, confess guilt, foul up, rail against senseless loss, pray for mercy, and seek comfort.

~ゔ

CHAPTER FOUR

Out of the Depths I Cry to You
Illness, Aging, and Other Serious Loss

Theologian Dorothee Soelle, the author of *Suffering*, describes three phases in the release from suffering. The first phase is characterized by muteness, isolation, and powerlessness; the second by lamenting and analyzing; and the third by organizing, overcoming powerlessness, and changing structures. The way out of suffering begins with finding a "language of lament, of crying, of pain, a language that at least says what the situation is" (70). Drawing on expressions in the psalms, Soelle considers lamenting to be indispensable in reaching the third stage, where change can occur (74). As we have already seen through the stories in the book, there are many kinds of pastoral care situations in which the psalms of disorientation can be an important element, in part because the psalmists speak out of their own condition of suffering, and we can readily see the movement from anguish to hope.

Addressing God takes the sufferer out of isolation; implicit in the act of lamenting by the psalmists is trust that they will come face to face with God, and God will come to them. Both act: the psalmist and God. Unwilling to settle for how things are, the psalmists pray, and they pray with the assumption that God will respond as a result of their complaints, accusations, and cajoling. In "Covenanting as Human Vocation: The Relation of the Bible and Pastoral Care" from *The Psalms and the Life of Faith*, Brueggemann writes, "Israel knew that such vigorous, even strident, grieving was an act of faithfulness. But it is crucial to note that the laments never focus long or finally on the object of loss. The speech may be about loss, but it is addressed to the God in whom Israel is grounded. Israel's primal scream is addressed to someone. Therefore, it has a chance of an answer" (160). This act of faithfulness has important implications for pastoral care to those who are suffering from illness and physical pain; depression; abandonment or betrayal by intimates, friends, or colleagues; self-inflicted or publicly mandated incarceration; abuse; dislocation from major life changes; and dissolution, such as of a marriage or employment.

Brueggemann says that pastoral care "means nurturing persons and community into a fresh metaphor that holds the possibility of making all things new" (165). Helping persons move into that fresh metaphor of possibility may require, as Soelle suggests, an act of lamenting by the sufferer. Expressing feelings in times of trouble, however, can be extremely difficult, and even impossible—for example, by someone who has lost the capacity to speak from a stroke or other cause. The psalms offer both a text for self-expression and a spiritual community for prayer that consists—at a minimum—of those praying, the psalmists, and God.

These connected ideas of Soelle and Brueggemann form the basis for the approach taken in this chapter. Chapter 3 laid a foundation for using psalms of disorientation in pastoral ministry to persons who are dying and bereaved. This chapter extends the discussion to additional pastoral situations that include ministry to those who are suffering from illness, aging, and the effects of other serious losses. Crying out of the pain is a step toward relief, empowerment, and needed change of the existing situation. The anguished appeal is made to God in faith, with confidence that God will respond, that transformation is possible. The paradox, discussed in chapter 3 in connection with terminally ill patients, is the implicit trust by those praying that change will occur, while giving up on an outcome—such as a cure for diabetes or that the eighty-year-old body will become as flexible as it was at thirty. This is not, however, to say that the "new situation created by the actions of God" excludes positive outcome; Brueggemann uses as a summary of the new situation this message Jesus sent to John the Baptist (Luke 7:22): "The blind receive their sight, the lame walk, the lepers are cleansed, the deaf hear, the dead are raised up, the poor have good news bought to them" (156–157). But the change that occurs through the movement of the psalm is an inner transformation for the individual or the community that offers the prayer. Two examples that illustrate this inner movement are Psalm 130 and Psalm 32.

Psalm 130
Out of the depths. I cry to you, O LORD.
Lord, hear my voice! Let your ears be attentive to the voice of my supplications!
If you, O Lord, should mark iniquities, Lord, who could stand?
But there is forgiveness with you, so that you may be revered.
I wait for the Lord, my soul waits, and in his word I hope;
my soul waits for the LORD more than those who watch for the morning,
more than those who watch for the morning.
O Israel, hope in the LORD!
For with the LORD there is steadfast love, and with him is great power to redeem.
It is he who will redeem Israel from all its iniquities.

Psalm 130 begins with a desperate cry to God from a place of peril and powerlessness. The psalmist then makes a theological point about how God operates—not, as some might think, keeping a strict record of human failings, because if that were the case, who would escape judgment? Instead, God forgives. From the depths, the speaker waits and hopes, which in the Old Testament are closely related, almost interchangeable terms, trusting that God's help is coming (Craven and Harrelson 876). The degree of hope offered by the psalmist is more even than that of someone who has stood watch through the dangers of the night and awaits the dawn. Beginning as one in deep darkness, the psalmist moves from cry to plea to hope, and by the end of the psalm is in a new situation, speaking for the entire community and expressing confidence that God will respond.

Psalm 32
Happy are those whose transgression is forgiven, whose sin is covered.
Happy are those to whom the LORD imputes no iniquity, and in whose spirit
there is no deceit.
While I kept silence, my body wasted away through my groaning all day long.
For day and night your hand was heavy upon me; my strength was dried up
as by the heat of the summer.
Then I acknowledged my sin to you, and I did not hide my iniquity; I said, "I
will confess my transgressions to the Lord," and you forgave the guilt of
my sin.
Therefore let all who are faithful offer prayer to you; at a time of distress, the
rush of mighty waters shall not reach them.
You are a hiding place for me; you preserve me from trouble; you surround
me with glad cries of deliverance.
I will instruct you and teach you the way you should go;
I will counsel you with my eye upon you.
Do not be like a horse or mule, without understanding, whose temper must be
curbed with bit and bridle, else it will not stay near you.
Many are the torments of the wicked, but steadfast love surrounds those who
trust in the LORD.
Be glad in the LORD and rejoice, O righteous, and shout for joy, all you
upright in heart.

In Psalm 32, the psalmist vividly describes the physical effect of keeping silent in a time of distress: "My body wasted away. . . . My strength was dried up as by the heat of the summer." The specific need is to make a confession of sin, which results in forgiveness. It is evident from the opening verses of the psalm that those who are happy (*ashre*: blessed, fortunate) are not those who are free of iniquity; sinfulness is assumed. Rather, those who are happy are those whose spirits are free of deceit—truthful to God, to others, and to themselves. Being happy, by implication in the following verses, involves not being bound by silence in times of struggle and chaos when the "mighty waters" rush and threaten us. Personal troubles, according to the psalmist, should be offered to God in prayer. Those who are faithful to God pray and receive protection from the turbulent waters. God provides not only sanctuary but help toward liberation, with glad cries of deliverance. The middle portion of the psalm contains instruction about the way to go, under God's watchful eye, as well as how not to go, like the horse or mule who needs to be reined in and controlled. The way to go is to trust in God. The psalmist has moved from a wasted body and all-day groaning to rejoicing and shouting for joy.

One patient with whom I was reading psalms erupted in anger after we read Psalm 32, saying in an emphatic tone, "I don't want to talk about sin. I've been beaten down enough by all of that. It's what I don't like about the psalms—they're so negative! Sin is what separates us from God, not all that wallowing in the 'I've been so bad' stuff." My immediate response was to be defensive, but fortunately I came to realize that this psalmist had moved beyond sin by speaking out loudly and clearly, and that's what the patient was doing as well.

I have heard a similar story about a priest who visited one of her parishioners in a nursing home. The patient didn't speak at all, or look at her, just stared ahead. The priest did not try to engage in small talk but instead picked up the psalms and began to read: 23, "The Lord is my shepherd," 121, "My help comes from the Lord, the maker of heaven and earth," and 131, "Like a child upon its mother's breast, my soul is quieted within me." Still getting no response, the priest "as a last resort" turned to the laments, and when she read from Psalm 102 about becoming "like a vulture in the wilderness, like an owl among the ruins . . . because you [God] have picked me up and tossed me aside, " the man's face softened, and he said, "Finally, somebody knows how I feel" (Davis 160–161). With my patient, the woman did her own protesting; in this instance, the psalmist made the anguished cries for the man, helping him move to new ground.

The psalmists also offer something else very important that society and the church often don't: they give a person permission to speak bluntly to God about unpleasant, sometimes reprehensible, feelings and desires. In a presentation on the psalms to a group of elderly women who suffered from a variety of health problems, including arthritis, diabetes, and the loss of hearing and eyesight., I used a handout on Psalm 3 to show them the structure of lament psalms:

Psalm 3 Structure of Laments

"O Lord" "O my God" (intimate address to God).

"How many are my foes! Many are rising up against me; many are saying to me, 'There is no help for you in God'" (what's wrong).

"Rise up," "Deliver me" (what's needed).

"For you strike all my enemies on the cheek; you break the teeth of the wicked" (desired vindication).

"You . . . are a shield around me, my glory, the one who lifts my head" (motivations for God).

"I cry aloud . . . and [God] answers me. . . . I lie down and sleep, I wake again, for

the Lord sustains me. I am not afraid of ten thousands of people who have set themselves against me all around" **(evidence of being heard)**.
"Deliverance belongs to the Lord; may your blessing be on your people!" **(doxology)**.

I used this format because I wanted them to see the psalmist's frankness about the problems, but also the faith in God that is so strong that there is no fear even of "thousands" against us. I wanted them to understand that enemies can be nonhuman, such as illness and addiction and natural disasters, and to point out that laments end not in a dark place but in praise. Although the women listened politely, many seemed more interested in the lemon chess pie that had been served for dessert. There were, however, a few sparks of connection, such as from one woman who especially liked the psalmists' down-to-earth use of flattery to get God to act. Another suggested the strong relationship between the psalms of struggle and horror to the recent tsunami disaster in Asia; the laments give us a voice of communal prayer. The most strongly expressed response, though, was made by a woman about the imprecations, the face striking and teeth breaking. She stood up at her table and said, "It is powerfully freeing just to know that I can say those things to God, that I don't have to hide them under this table or anywhere else!"

Intuition and Responsibility

Pastoral caregivers rely on their instincts to determine which spiritual resources will work, and those may change over the course of one visit or many. The priest who went into the nursing home to call on her male parishioner had a definite plan in mind to read comforting Scripture, but shifted abruptly during the course of the visit because of the patient's lack of response. The pastoral caregiver may have some information about a patient but has no way of knowing all that is in a person's life experience or spiritual reservoir and/or how Scripture might tap into that.

Hannah, a hospital chaplain, went in to visit a throat cancer patient, Mr. O'Brien, who had taken a sudden turn for the worse following surgery. Hannah knew very little about Mr. O'Brien other than the chart indicated he was Roman Catholic; but his situation seemed so drastic that she began to read Psalm 22, "My God, my God, why have you forsaken me? Why are you so far from helping me, from the words of my groaning?" By the time they got to the second verse, "O my God, I cry by day, but you do not answer; and by night, but find no rest," Mr. O'Brien had begun reciting the psalm with her—in Latin, which he'd memorized as a schoolboy. *Deus meus clamabo per diem et non exaudies et nocte ad insipientiam mihi.* He told Hannah in his raspy voice that this psalm gave him strength because it showed how Jesus, too, had cried out in desperation on the cross. They discussed the remainder of the psalm's message that God does not leave us in that place of desperation.

> But you, O LORD, do not be far away! O my help, come quickly to my aid!
> Deliver my soul from the sword, my life from the power of the dog!
> Save me from the mouth of the lion! From the horns of the wild oxen you
>   have rescued me....
> For [God] did not despise or abhor the affliction of the afflicted;
> he did not hide his face from me, but heard when I cried to him.
> From you comes my praise in the great congregation;
> my vows I will pay before those who fear him.
> The poor shall eat and be satisfied; those who seek [the LORD] shall praise the
>   LORD.
> May your hearts live forever! (vv. 19–21, 24–26)

This prayer for aid and comfort is strong in its insistence that God does not turn away or hide from those who are afflicted.

Hannah also ministered to Herb, a gay, HIV-positive man in his seventies who had come to the hospital from another town to receive treatment. He had requested a chaplain's visit because he wanted to reconnect with God and didn't know how to begin to pray. After an initial visit, Hannah copied out several psalms for him in large print so he could read them easily: 23, 27, 28, 31, 41, 121, and 139. They started reading the psalms together. Herb began to cry when they reached the middle section of Psalm 41:

> They think that a deadly thing has fastened on me, that I will not rise again
>   from where I lie.
> Even my bosom friend in whom I trusted, who ate of my bread, has lifted the
>   heel against me.
> But you, O Lord, be gracious to me, and raise me up, that I may repay them.
>   (vv. 8–10)

He talked about the horror of people's response to him, the fastening on to his body of a deadly thing that was so appalling to others. Then Herb told Hannah that his partner of many years had betrayed him and ended their relationship. It was something he had been unable to discuss. Hannah visited Herb several more times and says that he was clearly touched by finding his own story in the Scriptures, responding especially to the desperate feelings of "where is God?" expressed so clearly in some of the psalms.

Psalm 137

Three strikingly different responses, one strongly adverse, to Psalm 137 further illustrate the complexity of personal reactions to the psalms and the importance of a pastoral caregiver's sensitivity in selecting and communicating about them. Psalm 137 is a poem from exile following the destruction of Jerusalem in 587 B.C.E. by the Babylonian conquerors (2 Kgs. 25:8–12) who swept the people away after burning God's house, the houses of the people, and breaking down the walls of the city. Its last lines are probably the most troublesome in the book of Psalms, reflecting the depth and intensity of pain felt by those in exile.

Psalm 137

By the rivers of Babylon—there we sat down and there we wept when we
    remembered Zion.
On the willows there we hung up our harps.
For there our captors asked us for songs, and our tormentors asked us for
    mirth, saying, "Sing us one of the songs of Zion!"
How could we sing the LORD's song in a foreign land?
If I forget you, O Jerusalem, let my right hand wither!
Let my tongue cling to the roof of my mouth, if I do not remember you,
    if I do not set Jerusalem above my highest joy.
Remember, O LORD, against the Edomites the day of Jerusalem's fall, How
    they said, "Tear it down! Tear it down! Down to its foundations!"
O daughter Babylon, you devastator! Happy shall they be who pay you back
    what you have done to us!
Happy shall they be who take your little ones and dash them against the rock!

Sonya, a seminary professor, experienced family tragedy when her daughter-in-law was struck by a passenger car while carrying her two-and-a-half-month-old son in a baby carrier; she was thrust forward from the impact and fell, crushing the baby's head. Both mother and son survived, but the baby's injuries resulted in massive and permanent brain damage. The week following the accident, Sonya attended the noonday Eucharist at the seminary chapel, and during the service Psalm 137 was sung. When she saw the last lines coming—"Happy shall they be who pay you back what you have done to us! Happy shall they be who take your little ones and dash them against the rock!"—Sonya says she thought she was going to faint. She made it through the service but burst out of the chapel afterwards in tears. A priest on the faculty approached Sonya and invited her to talk. They went to a quiet place, and she said how upset she was that the liturgist hadn't omitted those verses about killing babies, bashing their heads, since the entire seminary community knew of her family's situation. After all, it was an option in the lectionary to omit them. She says the priest wanted to be helpful, but he didn't understand her response since the psalm was a part of the liturgy. All she could say was the baby's name, "Mason." He again said he was sorry but conveyed no understanding of her response. Sonya did not have the strength to explain any further, left, and went to her office and cried.

Beverly, an African American student at the same seminary, had a transforming experience in response to Psalm 137. Then in her mid-forties, Beverly was taking an Old Testament course in which the professor gave as an assignment reading and reflecting on this psalm. She says that something wonderful and amazing happened when she meditated on the psalm.

She found herself on the American shore with slaves, looking back on Africa; for the first time in her life she was standing with them, having a deep and visceral understanding of what it was like. In those moments she experienced her ancestors' history in America—plantation life, emancipation, sharecropping, migration north, juke joints. Coming through that history brought her up to her own life and especially the story of her grandmother who had worked for a wealthy white family. Beverly's grandmother adopted that family, in some ways abandoning her own. The psalm triggered intense anger, and Beverly admitted saying out loud, "I would bash that family's heads against the stone for stealing my grandmother." She came to see that mixed in with all of this sadness and anger was a sense of joy, "because it felt as though I became a part of my ancestors, my people, and African American history became a part of my life." From that experience Beverly came to a deeper understanding of the psalms and the permission God gives us to touch the dark and painful places in ourselves, not only permission but the vehicle to get there, to heal and transform. She felt that touching her own grief was a part of healing the history. "Inasmuch as we each can do that, individually and in community, we heal our history and we liberate ourselves to more fully enjoy our future."

Less dramatic but something that many of us experience in our lives, Teri's disorientation resulted from a geographic relocation, and her response to Psalm 137 is a common one to those affected in similar ways by a major move. When Teri left her home of more than twenty years to move to the desert area of Colorado's Western Slope for difficult personal reasons, she felt like a deeply rooted plant being pulled out of the ground. Teri's response to this psalm was to its overwhelming sense of melancholy, reflecting a deep longing for home, in the question, "How can we sing the Lord's song in a foreign land?" She describes herself as a person with a strong sense of place, grounded in relationships, church, and work. The move severed those connections, and Teri experienced "an incredible sense of disorientation in moving to a new community where I had no friends, no church home, no job, or even a permanent house." A visual artist, Teri's feelings of what she calls her "unrootedness" were so intense that her artwork for many months following the move was about roots. She wrote in her journal that in her former home, "I at least had garlic and onions, but in the desert, I have nothing." It felt like an exile and took a long time of "stumbling around in the dark" to reattach her roots. Psalm 137 was an important part of that process. Teri felt that God was largely absent from her during this period, and her spiritual director helped her see that the disruption in her faith life mirrored the rest of her life. But while she felt far *from* God, Teri was drawn *to* God through the psalmist's mournful cries of how hard it is to sing on alien soil. She recognized that what was happening to her had been happening to people for thousands of years. After living through the cycles of several seasons, Terry could begin to appreciate the smells, tastes, and sounds of her new home.

Conversation Patterns and the Psalms

In addition to the unique structure of laments, discussed above and in chapter 2, another distinct element makes them especially relevant to pastoral care. In Psalm 102, the speaker is suffering from severe illness, depression, grief, or a combination of maladies. The psalmist says of the symptoms: "For my days pass away like smoke, and my bones burn like a furnace. My heart is stricken and withered like grass; I am too wasted to eat my bread" (vv. 3–4). Along with its vivid expressions of an individual in distress, this psalm illustrates a structural characteristic of Hebrew poetry, which is the use of thought rhythms—called "parallelism"—rather than rhyme. Parallelism uses repetition for effect; the psalmist achieves a certain rhythm by speaking in successive phrases with slight variations each time. Parallelism occurs in two, sometimes three or more lines in relation to one another, and whole verses may be parallel to one another. There are many schemes for classifying the types of parallelism, but three commonly used types are illustrated in Psalm 102.

1. The second line essentially repeats the first, saying the same thing in a slightly different way (synonymous parallelism): "Hear my prayer"/"Let my cry come to you" (v. 1).
2. The second line contrasts with the first; a positive statement is echoed by a negative one in the other line (antithetic parallelism): "Do not hide your face from me in the day of my distress./Incline your ear to me; answer me speedily in the day when I call" (v. 2).
3. The second line adds or develops or completes the idea of the first (synthetic parallelism): "For my days pass away like smoke, and my bones burn like a furnace. . . ./Because of my loud groaning my bones cling to my skin" (vv. 3, 5).

While participating in a course for Clinical Pastoral Education, I realized that these patterns are similar to the way patients and family members sometimes speak in pastoral care settings. The Clinical Pastoral Education training requires the preparation of "verbatim" reports, based on patient visits, and are used for group discussion, critique, and feedback. They include some of the actual conversation between the patient and pastoral caregiver as well as notes on other aspects of the pastoral care visits. In my clinical assignment as a chaplain intern at a Veterans Administration hospital, I had visited short-term and long-term patients in a wide range of circumstances, and the verbatims show sections of conversation that mirror the thought-rhyming pattern of the psalms: (1) The patient or family member speaks and then echoes what she has just said with slight variations. (2) She speaks and then voices a contrasting thought, sometimes as if she is having an internal argument. (3) She speaks, often just as the chaplain is leaving, then adds to it a more complex or revealing statement, sometimes getting down to what she really wants to talk about. Here are two examples.

Example One: A cancer patient awaiting surgery made these comments at three points during my pre-surgical visit with her:

1. "I'm in God's hands. I'm being carried on this journey by God."

2. "I want to go back to school and become a teacher. I don't want to give up my dream."

3. "My spirit sometimes gets scared. It's telling me I won't get through this, I won't make it, or the surgery won't get all the cancer."

The follow-up discussion encouraged her to articulate her fears and to explore what she found helpful in confronting them.

Example Two: The grandson of a critically ill patient at the V.A. hospital made these comments during a visit the grandson had requested with a chaplain.

1. "I feel peaceful about things. I'm in a good place with all of this."

2. "My grandfather's body may fail, but he's not gonna leave me."

3. "My grandfather doesn't trust Jesus. If he doesn't believe in Jesus, he's going to hell."

In the follow-up conversation, he asked if I were "born again." I responded to his question by suggesting that he and I used a different language to talk about our faith. I agreed that his grandfather wasn't religious and didn't want prayers said, but he did like me to visit and impressed me as being a deeply spiritual man who valued and cared greatly for his family. The grandson eventually said he felt better about his grandfather's having some spiritual contact and that he wanted to get to know his grandfather better in the days they had remaining.

Pastoral caregivers will likely recognize these patterns of conversations. I provide them here to show another way in which the psalms might be helpful: by affirming the natural rhythms of the person who is speaking and his need to go over the same ground, often many times. Parallelism occurs throughout the psalms, and in other Old Testament Scripture, but the psalms of suffering and struggle are closely related to pastoral care dialogue because the patient or family member is discussing problems, revealing sometimes layer by layer in the process of talking what the difficulties are.

Another particular benefit of the parallelism in psalms of disorientation is that through them, the psalmist is able to convey empathy. One of the least helpful things that can be said to someone suffering from a painful affliction is, "I know how you are feeling," because no one truly does. The psalmist, however, is able to do exactly that, as the story of the nursing home patient illustrated. By praying these psalms with patients, the pastoral caregiver, too, is able to join in the psalmist's empathy.

Other Pastoral Care Applications

The pastoral issues that have been discussed in this and previous chapters—forgiveness of others, forgiveness of self, resolution of conflict, emotional release, relief from guilt—are relevant to many other kinds of major loss. The following are some additional examples of the many types of situations in which psalms of sorrow and suffering can be helpful in pastoral care. The potential impact of the psalm is an inner transformation; what propels movement is the honest expression of how things actually are and the turning to God with trust that God will hear and respond.

Aging

A gerontologist speaking to a group of pastoral caregivers told the story of Alma, an eighty-one-year-old woman. During the previous year Alma's husband of sixty-four years had died, and she moved across the country to live with her son and daughter-in-law, leaving behind her entire support base. Alma began experiencing some serious heart problems, along with an ongoing conflict with her daughter-in-law. The gerontologist pointed out that Alma's situation reflected losses that are common to the population of older adults. Alma needed to be encouraged and allowed to grieve her losses—to talk through her grief and to express herself through writing or other creative outlets. Alma's capacity to act and to accomplish things had become s greatly diminished, so more than ever she needed to know that she is valued for who she is now. It is important, too, to be aware that elderly adults can and do learn new things. Their patterns of learning may slow and change, but the capacity to learn continues. One of the extremely positive things that Alma has said in her sessions with the gerontologist is that her spiritual journey is taking her inward, allowing her to feel happier and more at peace in her own company.

The Rev. Barbara Cawthorne Crafton writes in *Meditations* on the Psalms, "People usually tiptoe around the central fact of an elderly person's life: that it's coming to an end," and that it is the younger person, not the older one, that has trouble with it. "I have found that many older people welcome a chance to talk about the end of life. That many of them are surprised by how much less fearsome a prospect it is to them, now that it is closer, than it used to be when they were younger. . . . We help each other immeasurably when we share our hopes and fears. There is no greater gift one human being can give another" (220). The psalms offer a prayerful forum for expressing the hopes and fears of aging. In Psalm 71, the psalmist is speaking from a time late in life:

> Do not cast me off in the time of old age; do not forsake me when my strength is spent. (v. 9)
>
> So even to old age and gray hairs, O God, do not forsake me. (v. 18)

The image of God in this psalm is one of refuge, and the prayer is spoken by one who has had a long-term relationship with God and acknowledges that there have been problems through life:

> In you, O LORD, I take refuge. . . . Be to me a rock of refuge, a strong fortress, to save me, for you are my rock and my fortress. (vv. 1, 3)
> Upon you I have leaned from my birth; it was you who took me from my mother's womb. . . . O God, from my youth you have taught me, and I still proclaim your wondrous deeds. (vv. 6, 17)
> You who have made me see many troubles. (v. 20)

The prayer, ultimately, is for revival and comfort:

> You . . . will revive me again; from the depths of the earth you will bring me up again. You will increase my honor, and comfort me once again. (vv. 20–21)

Psalm 4 deals with the isolation of those who are no longer dependent on what the world values: "You have put gladness in my heart more than when their grain and wine abound" (v. 7). What matters is the relationship with God, not the world's words or pleasures, "But know that the Lord has set apart the faithful" (v. 3), and the ultimate peace that comes from that relationship: "I will both lie down and sleep in peace; for you alone, O Lord, make me lie down in safety" (v. 8).

Psalm 90 also addresses the swift passing and difficulties of life: "You turn us back to dust. . . . The days of our life are seventy years, or perhaps eighty, if we are strong; even then their span is only toil and trouble; they are soon gone, and we fly away" (vv. 3, 10). The concern here is to make some sense of life as it nears its end, to find meaning in God's work as well as our own, and to provide for the generations to come:

> So teach us to count our days that we may gain a wise heart.
> Satisfy us in the morning with your steadfast love, so that we may rejoice and be glad all our days.
> Let your work be manifest to your servants, and your glorious power to their children.
> Let the favor of the Lord our God be upon us, and prosper for us the work of our hands—O prosper the work of our hands. (vv. 12, 14, 16–17)

What these psalms have in common is trust that God is present in the situation, hope that God will address the current needs—which encompass relief from spiritual, physical, and emotional distress—and faith that God will come to help us when we can no longer help ourselves.

Chronic and Degenerative Illness

In contrast to illness and injury from which we recover, a chronic disease, like the aging process, is continuing, and some diseases break the body down over time. Such health problems, in addition to the illness itself, may generate financial concerns that add to worry and anxiety, as well as the loss of independence, the loss of capacity to participate in favorite activities, the loss of considerable certainty, and the loss of the ability to do simple things—like tying a shoe or getting in and out of a chair without help— that others take for granted.

When he was in his forties, Mack's hands began to quiver, his handwriting changed from large-smooth to small-jerky, and his feet sometimes seemed glued to the floor. The ultimate diagnosis of Parkinson's disease left Mack at the age of forty-seven retired on disability due to the severity of his symptoms and the knowledge that his disease would progress. Faced with a multitude of complex changes in his life and choices about how to live it, Mack found that the questions raised in Psalm 13 were similar to the ones he was asking:

> How long, O LORD? Will you forget me forever? How long will you hide your face from me?
> How long must I bear pain in my soul, and have sorrow in my heart all day long?
> How long shall my enemy be exalted over me? (vv. 1–2)

The psalmist's situation was related to his own, even, Mack says laughing, complete with the shaking:

> Consider and answer me, O *Lord* my God! Give light to my eyes, or I will sleep the sleep of death, and my enemy will say, "I have prevailed"; my foes will rejoice because I am shaken. (vv. 3–4)

The movement made in the psalm offered an objective in prayer that Mack believed to be desirable:

> But I trusted in your steadfast love; my heart shall rejoice in your salvation.
> I will sing to the LORD, because he has dealt bountifully with me. (vv. 5–6)

The psalmist proceeds on the assumption that God has dealt bountifully whatever hand has been dealt; for the twenty years since his diagnosis, Mack has proceeded on that assumption as well. Using his background in the printing industry, he helped establish a graphics communication course for the Texas Department of Corrections that has lowered the recidivism rate among inmates completing the program. He has worked in Habitat for Humanity, been active in his church, and made a difference to his community by founding a support group for persons with Parkinson's. Initially a group of 5 men called the Movers and Shakers, the group has since expanded to 140 members, about evenly divided between those with the disease and those who come as caregivers. During the twenty years Mack has lived with Parkinson's, he has had five surgeries, and 3 of the original members of Movers and Shakers have died. He is currently grieving the death of both parents within the last year. Along with other psalms and Scripture, Mack continues to rely on Psalm 13 because the questions recur, as they do for anyone suffering from long-term illness; so do the responses and assumptions about how God deals with us.

Divorce

Irene participates in both a bereavement support group and a divorce support group. One is to grieve the death of her mother, the other because her husband filed for divorce and custody of their daughter shortly after her mother's death. Some members of the divorce group have suggested that grieving for a divorced spouse is similar to grieving a death, but Irene disagrees. What she feels about her mother's death is sadness and a sense of abandonment; about the divorce, she feels vengeful fury at her husband and no confidence in herself. While the process of grieving may be similar—in both cases, the desired movement is toward restoring balance and reclaiming one's life—Irene's complicated grief underscores what is for her a vast difference between losing a loved one from death and losing a relationship with a loved one who is still living.

Some emotions, such as anger, are common to almost anyone going through divorce or the breakup of a long-term committed relationship. In Psalm 70 (and Ps. 40:13–17) the speaker combines feelings of rage and revenge:

> Let those be put to shame and confusion who seek my life.
> Let those be turned back and brought to dishonor who desire to hurt me.
> Let those who say "Aha, Aha!" turn back because of their shame (Ps. 70:2–3)

while praying to God for deliverance,

> Be pleased, O God, to deliver me. . . .
> You are my help and my deliverer; O Lord, do not delay! (vv. 1, 5)

Psalm 73 places the arrogant and wicked in slippery places, falling to ruin (v. 18), while the troubled speaker receives God's support and counsel:

> When my soul was embittered, when I was pricked in heart, I was stupid and
>   ignorant;
> I was like a brute beast toward you.
> Nevertheless I am continually with you; you hold my right hand.
> You guide me with your counsel, and afterward you will receive me with
>   honor. (vv. 21–24)

The anguished speaker in Psalm 69 pleads for God's help: "Save me, O God, for the waters have come up to my neck. I sink in deep mire, where there is no foothold" (vv. 1–2), turning to God because God manifests abundant and steadfast love, no matter what the person has said or done: "O God, you know my folly; the wrongs I have done are not hidden from you. . . . My prayer is to you, O Lord. At an acceptable time, O God, in the abundance of your steadfast love, answer me" (vv. 5, 13). Another psalm that offers personal affirmation is Psalm 139:* "For it was you who

---

* Ps. 139 includes clearly expressed imprecations of enemies against God in vv. 19–20 but like many other mixed psalms does not fall neatly into any classification category. I used it in chapter 3 as an example of a comfort psalm. Holladay points out that Ps. 139 is variously considered "a hymn, an individual song of thanksgiving and confidence, a declaration of innocence, and a didactic (wisdom) psalm" (69), while Shepherd classifies Ps. 139 as an individual lament (16).

formed my inward parts; you knit me together in my mother's womb. I praise you, for I am fearfully and wonderfully made. Wonderful are your works; that I know very well" (vv. 13–14). Other psalms that are helpful in dealing with emotions triggered by divorce and separation include 31, 51, 54, 55, and 56, as the following personal stories illustrate.

Ella, feeling that her life was in chaos after the divorce from her husband of more than twenty years, desperately needed a shoring up of inner strength but also a sense of outer protection. She found support in Psalm 31's images of God as "rock and my fortress" (v. 2). What also helped was the psalmist's encouragement to trust in God's plan: "But I trust in you, O Lord; I say, 'You are my God.' My times are in your hand; deliver me from the hand of my enemies and persecutors" (vv. 14–15). The psalm also reinforced her belief that God will work things out in God's time: "Be strong, and let your heart take courage, all you who wait for the Lord" (v. 24).

Daniel sought a divorce after he fell in love with another man and accepted that he was gay. Although he believed he had made an emotionally and spiritually healthy decision, and for many years has shared a life with his male partner, Daniel felt enormous guilt following the divorce because he had broken sacred marital vows. He prayed Psalm 51 daily for many months:

> Have mercy on me, O God, according to your steadfast love;
> according to your abundant mercy blot out my transgressions.
> Wash me thoroughly from my iniquity, and cleanse me from my sin.
> For I know my transgressions and my sin is ever before me.
> Against you only have I sinned and done what is evil in your sight. . . .
> Create in me a clean heart, O God, and put a new and right spirit within me.
> Do not cast me away from your presence and do not take your holy spirit
>   from me.
> Restore to me the joy of your salvation, and sustain in me a willing spirit. (vv.
>   1–4; 10–12)

Daniel's priest helped him understand fully that "the sacrifice acceptable to God is a broken spirit; a broken and contrite heart, O God, you will not despise" (Ps. 51:17). During the following Lenten season, Daniel focused his prayer of confession at each Sunday Eucharist on the events and decisions that troubled him from the divorce, and finally he was able to receive and accept forgiveness.

Janet experienced tremendous anxiety in the aftermath of her divorce and relied on the monthly child support she received from her former husband for their three children. After two years, he began skipping payments and eventually moved to Canada in order to avoid the payments altogether. She found herself wishing for revenge and relied on psalms, such as Psalm 54, to help vent her rage:

> Save me, O God, by your name, and vindicate me by your might.
> Hear my prayer, O God; give ear to the words of my mouth.

For the insolent have risen against me, the ruthless seek my life; they do not
   set God before them.
But surely, God is my helper; the Lord is the upholder of my life.
He will repay my enemies for their evil. In your faithfulness, put an end to
   them. (vv. 1–5)

Janet also prayed Psalm 56, calling out to God for help in dealing with all of her "enemies": "Be gracious to me, O God, for people trample on me; all day long foes oppress me; my enemies trample on me all day long, for many fight against me. O Most High, when I am afraid, I put my trust in you" (vv. 1–2). Working though these emotions helped Janet take necessary financial and legal steps to move on in her life.

After his wife sued for divorce Dave wanted only escape so that he would not have to deal with "the who did what to whom and why and what was going to happen next." When things were at their worst, he meditated on Psalm 55: "And I say, 'O that I had wings like a dove! I would fly away and be at rest; truly, I would flee far away; I would lodge in the wilderness'" (vv. 6–7), visualizing himself actually flying away, which provided temporary escape. He appreciated that the psalmist's problems included betrayal in a relationship: "My companion laid hands on a friend and violated a covenant with me with speech smoother than butter, but with a heart set on war; with words that were softer than oil, but in fact were drawn swords" (vv. 20–21). Verse 22 helped Dave turn back to God: "Cast your burden on the Lord, and he will sustain you; he will never permit the righteous to be moved."

Loss of Employment

People who have lost jobs often feel rejected and betrayed by their former employers, and regardless of why the job loss has occurred or at what level of employment, many experience a profound sense of failure. When prospects for obtaining another job are bleak, their reaction is even stronger. In Psalm 143, the enemy has crushed "my life to the ground, making me sit in darkness like those long dead. Therefore my spirit faints within me; my heart within me is appalled" (vv. 3–4). Here, the psalmist prays for guidance in what to do next. "Let your good spirit lead me on a level path" (v. 10), but is brutally honest about what to do to those who have caused the damage: "In your steadfast love cut off my enemies, and destroy all my adversaries, for I am your servant" (v. 12).

Paul was laid off from his position as a mechanical engineer at a Fortune 500 company during an economic downturn. The financial press regularly carried stories about the firm's outstanding financial performance during a period when most of its competitors were struggling. What press accounts did not reveal was the tremendous human cost of financial decisions that allowed the company to succeed. One step is outsourcing—

moving manufacturing operations to third-world countries where labor costs are lower and payment of benefits is usually unnecessary. The other major cost-savings step has been to replace middle managers and other professional employees with newly hired college graduates at much lower salaries. There are benefits for some, such as foreign workers and young people in the workforce, but many like Paul have lost a great deal as the firm continues to lay off employees in small groups so as not to attract press attention. A helpful psalm for Paul's situation is Psalm 26. We do not know what has occurred in this psalm, but the psalmist mounts a personal defense: "Vindicate me, O Lord, for I have walked in integrity, and I have trusted in the Lord without wavering. . . . I wash my hands in innocence" (vv. 1, 6). Up against sinners and the bloodthirsty, "those in whose hands are evil devices and whose right hands are full of bribes" (v. 10), the prayer is for God's redemption and graciousness: "Redeem me, and be gracious to me" (v. 11). Some of the lessons learned from Paul's story and from many recent company failures, where people have lost not only employment but life's savings, reflect a corporate environment of greed in which some companies use tactics which—even if legal—are often questionable on moral and ethical grounds. Psalm 26 reminds us that this environment is not new, and that the individual caught in this atmosphere has choices. The psalmist chooses a path of personal integrity: "But as for me, I walk in my integrity. . . . My foot stands on level ground" (vv. 11–12).

A Lutheran church in the Texas community where I lived for many years has developed a Scripture study course that helps readers respond to God through the psalms out of the human experience of pain as well as joy (Peace Lutheran). One of the psalms covered in the course is Psalm 88, which has as a theme the feeling of being cut off and in a place where there is no strength or hope:

> I am counted among those who go down to the Pit; I am like those who have
>   no help,
> like those forsaken among the dead, like the slain that lie in the grave,
> like those whom you remember no more, for they are cut off from your hand.
> You have put me in the depths of the Pit, in the regions dark and deep.
> Your wrath lies heavy upon me, and you overwhelm me with all your waves.
> You have caused my companions to shun me; you have made me a thing of
>   horror to them.
> I am shut in so that I cannot escape; my eye grows dim through sorrow.
> Every day I call on you, O Lord; I spread out my hands to you. (vv. 4–9)

The course text suggests that that this could be the prayer of anyone facing the reality of unemployment as well as other situations (famine, poverty, the threat of terrorism). Unlike other laments, this one does not move from anguish to praise; the psalmist's plea goes unanswered. In this kind of despair, it is hard for the one praying to feel any closeness to God—

with its images of darkness, suffocation, anger, rejection, and terror. The speaker questions what God has done, "O Lord, why do you cast me off? Why do you hide your face from me?" (v. 14). There are times when the only authentic communication with God is the bluntly honest admission of feeling abandoned and left in a grim place. But at the same time, the psalmist's plea, "O Lord, God of my salvation, when, at night, I cry out in your presence, let my prayer come before you; incline your ear to my cry" (v. 1–2), is an act of trust in God.

Then I Spoke with My Tongue

Most laments end in praise, but some do not, as we have seen in the above example from Psalm 88. Neither does Psalm 39, which ends with the speaker's desire to be left alone by God. "Turn your gaze away from me" (v. 13). In this psalm, the speaker states, "LORD, let me know my end, and what is the measure of my days; let me know how fleeting my life is" (v. 4). Helpless and distressed, this psalmist recognizes that the end of life is coming—"You have made my days a few handbreadths, and my lifetime is as nothing in your sight" (v. 5)—and that our time on God's earth is temporary, "I am your passing guest" (v. 12). The core question, however, comes in the middle of the psalm:

> And now, O LORD, what do I wait for? My hope is in you.
> Deliver me from all my transgressions. Do not make me the scorn of the fool.
> I am silent; I do not open my mouth, for it is you who have done it.
> Remove your stroke from me; I am worn down by the blows of your hand.
> You chastise mortals in punishment for sin, consuming like a moth what is dear to them;
> surely everyone is a mere breath.
> Hear my prayer, O LORD, and give ear to my cry; do not hold your peace at my tears.
> For I am your passing guest, an alien, like all my forbears. (vv. 7–12)

The psalmist makes clear that our confidence and security come not from humans, who are a "mere breath," or in things heaped up—"They heap up, and do not know who will gather" (v. 6)—but from God. *My hope is in you.* What do I wait for? *My hope is in you.* Echoing the theme that began the chapter, this psalmist offers a reason for why we should not keep silent before God in our times of trouble: "I was silent and still; I held my peace to no avail; my distress grew worse" (v. 2). This overt expression of the need to lament together with the psalmist's recognition that darkness ("I am worn down by the blows of your hand") can coexist with hope are the places to start in identifying with those who are suffering and in helping begin the journey out of isolation toward healing and new orientation. *Hear my prayer. Give heed to my cry. Do not hold your peace at my tears.*

ॐ

CHAPTER FIVE

Like a Lonely Bird on the Housetop
Adolescence and the Psalms

All wearing crew cuts, khaki pants with an elastic waist, and short-sleeved polo shirts, Stephen, Raul, Derek, Jesse, Jim, and Gerald arrived for the first class. David followed a couple of minutes later, not allowed to enter the classroom until he was frisked at the door by a staff member. These seven young men, ages seventeen and eighteen, comprised my first creative writing class at the county youth detention facility. The class began as the outgrowth of an ongoing hospice program to help incarcerated youth deal with the many losses in their lives, such as the death of family members and close friends; family breakups from divorce, separation, and parental incarceration; multiple geographic moves and school changes; addictions and health-related issues; and for all of them, the loss of freedom. The hospice group leader found that most participants had difficulty communicating their feelings, and any opportunities she gave them for creative expression helped open things up.

The group met for one hour on Tuesdays for grief support, and we added another hour on Thursdays for this creative writing class. I had no knowledge of the reasons for their confinement other than the statistics in the newspaper showing that the largest percentages of crimes committed by those detained in this facility are related to drug and sex offenses. Eventually, some of the students wrote bits that provided clues, such as about drug addiction and a gun "going off" at a party, resulting in a death.

After the hospice staff member introduced me, I started that first session by telling them something about my background as a writer and college teacher—although what interested the students the most was that I had a daughter who worked for Universal Studios in Los Angeles. I then asked about their interest in writing and reading. Several had studied for and passed the G.E.D. exam while incarcerated, and everyone in the class expressed some desire to write—stories, lyrics, rap, poetry. Jim confidently stated his intention to write a novel. Most regularly checked out books from the facility's library, and they seemed to like a huge range of authors, from Poe and Shelly to Nevada Barr, Bill Bryson, and Mario Puzo.

I explained that we would use some of the class time to discuss writing examples from literature, but there would also be ample time for them to write on their own. Jesse quickly asked, "Is it okay to write about bad stuff?" I assured them that their work in the class was confidential and gave them a simple set of class writing rules: keep your hand moving, write what you want, write honestly, and don't criticize yourself. For the first class, I provided a list of suggested writing topics, which most used, but in subsequent classes they usually came up with an idea of their own or continued writing about what they had already begun. At the end of each session, I collected the work and then returned the folders at the start of the next class. When the class finished, they lined up silently at the door and walked, under supervision, to their next classroom. Every time they moved anywhere within the facility, they did so with their hands clasped behind them.

During the initial class meeting, they had about fifteen minutes to write freely, after which those who wanted could read their work to the class. Everyone began writing immediately and kept going until I said time was up, and all were eager to share their work, although we ran out of time before two of the students could read. When I asked at the next class if those two would like to read, Raul had already removed his paper from the folder, wadded it up, and thrown it into the trash. I said I thought his piece was interesting and would be glad to retrieve it if he wanted to read it to the class. He said in a confrontational tone, *"You read it?"* and I thought, *Uh-oh, this is trouble.* I explained that I had read all of the students' writing, but if there was work someone didn't want me to read, to let me know. It turned out that Raul was not upset that I had read his work, but simply surprised that anyone would be interested in something he wrote. Raul retrieved, unwadded, and read the piece, a poem called "Love and Hate" about what is left of us after we die—emotions, memories, and thoughts that remain suspended in time and space. In that first class we had discussed a contemporary poem by Nikki Giovanni and had talked about how modern poets often link the lines through related sounds and alliteration rather than perfect rhyme. Gerald commented that Raul's work was like that. Raul said, "I hadn't noticed, but when I read the poem out loud I could hear those sounds," and he was obviously pleased with the attention and response.

Throughout the sessions the students were attentive and respectful, but they still managed to find ways to tease me. On one of the class days, three students, smiling broadly, came in wearing different uniforms: yellow short-sleeved cotton pullover shirts with matching yellow pants, similar to hospital scrubs. "How do you like our new look?" Jim asked, beaming proudly, and I complimented their outfits, telling them how "cool" they looked. I subsequently learned when they returned to the standard khaki-polo shirt combination that these yellow suits had actually been a major step down, symbolizing the removal of privileges for disciplinary reasons.

We began each of the classes with a discussion of literature—a poem or a short prose piece—which they seemed to enjoy. For two of the classes, I decided to use excerpts from psalms of suffering along with other poetry because I was interested in seeing how the students would relate to these psalms within the context of other works of classic literature, and I also wanted to try out use of the psalms in a nonreligious setting. The first handout included the following portions of Psalm 102:

> I am like an owl of the wilderness,
> like a little owl of the waste place
> I lie awake; I am like a lonely bird on the housetop.
> All day long my enemies taunt me;
> those who deride me use my name for a curse.
>
> [God] will regard the prayer of the destitute.
>
> Long ago you laid the foundations of the earth,
> and the heavens are the work of your hands.
>
> You are the same, and your years have no end.
> The children of your servants shall live secure;
> their offspring shall be established in your presence. (vv. 6–8, 17, 25, 27–28)

The other three poems were "We Wear the Mask" by Paul Laurence Dunbar, "The Lake Isle of Innisfree" by William Butler Yeats, and "Sonnet 29" by William Shakespeare. I tried to select works that were related in some way to themes of disorientation in the psalm (internal strife, isolation, desire for inner peace, concern with what others are saying, self-pity, outcast state). During the discussions, I said very little other than to answer questions, clarify terms, and provide dates so that they would be aware of the range of periods represented by the poetry, from ancient to modern.

We began by reading aloud the Dunbar poem, which is about wearing a mask to hide feelings. *Why should the world be over-wise/In counting all our tears and sighs?/Nay, let them only see us while we wear the mask/We smile, but, O great Christ, our cries/To thee from tortured souls arise.* There was general agreement that this poet was describing how the boys themselves dealt with problems in detention: that it is essential to have a mask for outer protection of what they are feeling inside. Derek later wrote an essay, "Why I Don't Want to Act Smart and Show My True Colors."

The initial reaction to Yeats's leaving the world behind was confusion: *I will arise and go now, and go to Innisfree/ . . . for peace comes dropping slow/Dropping from the veils of morning to where the cricket sings/There midnight's all a glimmer, and noon a purple glow/And evening full of the Linnet's wings.* Jim said, "What is this guy talking about?" but with more discussion, they decided it was a poem about sanctuary, and every student was able to describe a peaceful place that he had regularly visited as a personal sanctuary: e.g., a park in East St. Louis; an area behind the high school in Nashua, New Hampshire; a local site called the "Potholes"; a trail in the mountains in Utah.

The Shakespearean sonnet also produced in initial confusion. *Beweep my outcast state/And trouble deaf heaven with bootless cries/ . . . Featured like him, like him with friends possessed.* But they kept reading and pondering: *Haply I think on thee, and then my state/Like to the lark at break of day arising/From sullen earth, sings hymns at heaven's gate.* Jesse said, "This guy wants to sing like a lark," and Stephen added, "He's just talking about what really matters: his girlfriend." *For thy sweet love remembered such wealth brings.* Everybody laughed, and nodded agreement, impressed that together they had figured it out.

In response to the psalm, Gerald said, "There are repetitions, like saying 'owl, owl, lonely bird'; then 'of the wilderness' and 'of the waste places.'" I asked why he thought the poet did that, and he said, "It doesn't rhyme—they're doing this repeating instead." I wanted to stand and applaud his insight—quickly picking up the use of parallelism, which is a hallmark of Hebrew poetry, the rhythmic pattern of repetition. David commented on the connections among the poems—Dunbar's writing about wearing a mask, Yeats's about getting away from it all, and "this guy turning to heaven, turning to God when there's trouble." Jim said, "He just feels sorry for himself," but Jim also commented that loneliness and taunting were common problems for him in his life in detention: "That's what we have in here all the time." Jesse said he could relate to the psalmist's way of dealing with things, even though it was probably a good idea to hide it. "I mean, like saying a prayer when things are hard is a way of communicating when no other communication is possible, and that's what it's like in here. Sometimes it's all I have. That's tight, but I wouldn't want most of the people here to know it."

This was the best discussion, the most open and free-flowing, that we had during the entire course. The students amazed themselves with their ability to "get it," to "get" what the poets were saying in their strange language that had seemed so enigmatic. There was a sense of relief to be able to admit to something so vulnerable as the desire to pray, which discussing the psalm allowed them to do. I think our discussion benefited too from the fact that we weren't meeting in our regular classroom where we sat on high stools at metal tables. On this particular day our classroom was in use for a staff meeting, so we were moved to a lounge area, where we sat in comfortable chairs in an oval arrangement with no table at all. It wasn't as good a setup for the writing portion of the class but was very conducive to a group conversation that felt as if some barriers had been removed, and the class members were at least temporarily open to new ways of looking at the world: through the eyes of the psalmist and other poets. In his article "A Working Theology of Prison Ministry," prison chaplain Stephen T. Hall writes that prior to incarceration many inmates have grown up in an atmosphere of dysfunctional families and peer groups that are involved in antisocial behavior. Inmates encounter these same kinds of patterns in prison because of the nature of where they are. "For them to grow in their personal development and reduce the chances that they will repeat past patterns, it is essential to be shown a different way of relating to the world around them" (173–174). That's what I wanted to happen from our study of literature and involvement in the creative writing process—that their way of seeing the world would change, just as our group dynamic was transformed by altering the class's setting and seating.

For the following week's class, I developed a handout on the theme of choices using "Harlem" by Langston Hughes, "The Road Not Taken" by Robert Frost, a section of Shakespeare's *Hamlet* with Polonius's advice to Laertes, and excerpts from Psalm 90:

> For a thousand years in your sight
> are like yesterday when it is past,
> or like a watch in the night.
>
> The days of our life are seventy years,
> Or perhaps eighty if we are strong;
> even then their span is only toil and trouble;
> they are soon gone, and we fly away.
>
> So teach us to count our days
> that we may gain a wise heart.
>
> And prosper for us the work of our hands—
> O prosper the work of our hands! (vv. 4, 10, 12, 17)

We started the discussion with "Harlem," which begins with the question, "What happens to a dream deferred?" and after reading through the poem, *"Does it dry up/like a raisin in the sun?/Or fester like a sore—/And then run?/. . .Maybe it just sags/like a heavy load./Or does it explode?"* I asked what they thought it meant to have a dream deferred. Gerald said the answer was in Derek's drawing. Several of the students doodled and drew during the creative writing classes as well as in the grief group, and Derek had created a drawing that he called 'Time Lost," with numerals representing his four years of incarceration, a large clock, and images of a wooden fence and a low brick wall reflecting the world outside. We looked together at his art and agreed with Gerald's observation.

About Frost's familiar poem "The Road Not Taken," Stephen said, "We think we can go back, but often we can't. The path we take now is the only one we'll have." Much of Stephen's work in the class was on an essay that he called "The Cities of My Life," in which he wrote and diagrammed routes to the cities of "Success" and "Ghetto," and Ghetto's suburbs "Prison" and "Death." He wanted to take the difficult road to "Success," but in spite of multiple attempts, he wrote that he had been unable to do so. Jesse said he had a plaque on his bedroom wall at home with the quotation from Shakespeare, "This above all: to thine own self be true," that his father had given him, and it was a reminder to be himself, no matter what his friends were doing or trying to get him to do.

Although the discussion of the psalm was not as extensive as the week before, the comments were interesting. Gerald said he read the psalms a lot, and he liked them because "they are complicated." I asked him what that meant, and he said, "They go back and forth, more like life, not just in a straight line getting smoothly from here to there." Raul said, "And this one's saying don't get down on yourself while you're going bumpety-bump along the path." "Yeah," Jim added, "We're all going to die, so let's do something useful." "Like now," Stephen said. "We need to do it now."

Using the Psalms with Youth

The psalms can be especially helpful to adolescents because they reflect many of the personal problems and challenges that youth encounter. Adolescents struggle with such issues as grief from the death of parents, other family members, friends, or pets; the loss of their families from divorce and separation; betrayals; emotional and physical bullying; academic stress; confusion about sex; fear of pregnancy; addictions and eating disorders; gang violence; and suicide attempts. Some youth ministers say that they rely on the psalms as a resource because the teens identify, in ways that they often can't in other parts of Scripture, with the psalmists' expressions of emotions that seem similar to what they are experiencing: anger, fear, depression, jealousy, alienation, confusion, humiliation, loneliness, and the intense desire for revenge. A teenager can identify with the psalmist's anger at enemies—"their mouth is full of cursing, deceit, and oppression"—and fear of abandonment—"darkness is my only companion."

Mike, the youth minister at a large suburban church, says that teenagers' biggest problem is the same one that my students in the detention center have: they don't think they can talk about what is really bothering them. Relatively small issues that might be resolved through conversation become huge, and huge issues such as a pregnancy scare grow to gigantic proportions. Mike believes that the alienation his teens suffer is not alienation from God but from the world. Adults tell them, "You'll understand this later when you're older," sending a message that young people are somehow not competent to express themselves. They don't know they can say things about how they are feeling and why they are scared or upset about it. The psalms can help because the psalmists tell God, without holding anything back, about what's really going on in their lives.

Marcella finally came to Mike because she had no one else to tell that she had missed two monthly periods and feared she was pregnant. She couldn't tell her friends because they would think she was a whore. She couldn't talk to her parents because they would be furious and disappointed and let down and ashamed. James can't be himself around his friends because he fears they will ostracize him for not being attracted to girls. He senses his emotions are different. Like Marcella, he doesn't feel he can talk to his parents or his peers. At school, Kelly has been labeled "weird," and she experiences daily emotional distress as a result. Roger, who was in the church youth group, says that being in the group carries with it the expectation that you don't drink, use drugs, or have sex. Now that he does two out of three, Roger no longer believes he can be involved in the church, that he has excluded himself. Jennifer's parents have recently divorced. She feels abandoned by both parents and believes she caused their split.

Mike tells these teens to stand strong, to be honest, to open up. He encourages them to read the psalms because that is what the psalmists do: open up to God, expressing honest emotions, often from the midst of some of their worst crises. In his article, "Who Do You Say That I Am?" youth minister Stuart Brooks Keith III writes, "We minister most faithfully when we facilitate a young person's encounter with the living God" (28). Praying these psalms is to encounter the living God, often from the depths of despair.

The teenage years are a time of breaking away from the family of origin and making one's way as an individual. When this process is interrupted by the death of someone significant, such as a sibling or a grandparent, the process of separating is interrupted by intense grief. Adolescents may also experience resentment at being drawn back into the family circle as part of the grief process, assuming new roles, or revising life plans. They may feel like their lives must suddenly change course: "Should I go away to college or stay home with the family?" A teen may see herself as the parent figure for younger siblings because the surviving adult parent is immersed in grief, or she may have an older sibling who assumes the parent role, which can cause another kind of authority struggle. A teenager who turns to peers at this time in her life is probably seeking support and information from others who have never experienced a similar loss. Friends can lose patience with her because she is not "getting back to normal," while she might also lose patience with friends who become upset over such "minor" problems as a bad exam grade or not being invited to the prom. School can be an enormous challenge to grieving teenagers because they find it difficult to concentrate, and teachers may not recognize the level of distress. Young people who have suffered a great loss want support but not attention. They may turn to unhealthy coping mechanisms such as drugs and alcohol. Risky behavior at this time is normal, but grieving teens may make statements such as, "Why not take chances? My mom did everything right and she died."

The psalms can help young people know that they are not alone in their misery, and they encourage the reader—rather than acting out of difficult emotions, such as anger and intense desire for revenge—to take these feelings to God in prayer. The following is a list of psalms with relevant themes for some common adolescent problems. In addition to praying and singing and discussing the theology of these psalms, some youth groups have developed skits based on their content; written psalms of their own; made checklists in which they mark places in the psalm that match the feelings of them or their friends or family members; used the psalms in relation to a difficult current issue in the news by finding a psalm that fits the problem or turning the news event into a psalm of its own; and used the psalm's themes to create a collaborative psalm in which one person starts, the next person adds a verse, and so on until everyone has contributed a verse.

Some Expressions in the Psalms that Relate to Teen Issues (Book of Common Prayer):

Psalm 3 *Being "picked on" by others*
How many adversaries I have! How many there are who rise up against me! How many there are who say of me, "There is no help for you in God."

Psalm 6 *Grief*
Every night I drench my bed and flood my couch with tears. My eyes are wasted with grief.

Psalm 10 *Bullies*
Why do you stand so far off, O Lord, and hide yourself in time of trouble? Their mouth is full of cursing, deceit, and oppression; under their tongue are mischief and wrong.

Psalm 22 *Suffering from abuse, feelings of abandonment; addiction*
My God, my God, why have you forsaken me? and are so far from my cry and from the words of my distress? O my God, I cry in the daytime, but you do not answer; by night as well, but I find no rest.

Psalm 31 *Sorrow; grief; problems having physical effect*
Have mercy on me, O Lord, for I am in trouble; my eye is consumed with sorrow, and also my throat and belly. For I have heard the whispering of the crowd.

Psalm 35 *Desire for revenge*
Fight those who fight me, O Lord; attack those who are attacking me.
Let their way be dark and slippery.

Psalm 44 *Humiliation*
My humiliation is daily before me, and shame has covered my face.

Psalm 55 *Desire for escape*
And I said, "Oh, that I had wings like a dove! I would fly away and be at rest. I would flee to a far-off place and make my lodging in the wilderness. I would hasten to escape from the stormy wind and tempest."

Psalm 69 *Feeling overwhelmed*
Save me, O God, for the waters have risen up to my neck. I am sinking in deep mire, and there is no firm ground for my feet.

Psalm 73 *Envy of others*
Because I envied the proud and saw the prosperity of the wicked: For they suffer no pain, and their bodies are sleek and sound. In the misfortunes of others they have no share; they are not afflicted as others are.

Psalm 102 *Intense loneliness*
I am like a sparrow, lonely on a house-top.

Psalm 143 *Need for trust and guidance*
Let me hear of your loving-kindness in the morning, for I put my trust in you; show me the road that I must walk, for I lift up my soul to you. Teach me to do what pleases you, for you are my God; let your good Spirit lead me on level ground.

Hilary, who works with teens at her church and who has a seventeen-year-old daughter, believes that the psalms provide a model of candor for young people because the psalmists are not afraid to cry out and to trust God, to tell God what's in their hearts, sometimes as simply as asking, "How long, O God, how long?" She likens teenagers to members of the bird kingdom. They don't want to let the rest of the flock know that there's anything wrong. If they do, they'll be ostracized or pecked to death. Adolescents need to find that safe zone where God's grace can come in and help, so the flock doesn't run them off. She especially likes to use Psalm 139 with middle school and high school students:

Where can I go then from your Spirit? where can I flee from your presence?
If I climb up to heaven, you are there; if I make the grave my bed, you are
      there also.
If I take the wings of the morning and dwell in the uttermost parts of the sea,
Even there your hand will lead me and your right hand hold me fast. (vv. 6–9)

This psalm gives them a sense of God's presence, the awareness that we are never alone.

A Ministry of Affirmation

All of the young men from my class at the Youth Detention Center were in a profound state of disorientation, triggered by and leading to multiple upheavals in their lives and the lives of those affected by their crimes. Other stories in the book have demonstrated instances in which one or more of the psalms has helped turn a key, leading to release and the beginning of movement out of disorientation and toward recovery. The next step for many of the incarcerated youth is a different kind of release—to some sort of halfway house, with tight supervision but less restriction, and jobs in the community. All but one of the students from my class who have been released thus far have ultimately returned to some form of detention, either the youth facility or the adult jail. Is there any sense in which we can say that the psalms—together with the study of other literature and involvement in the creative process—have given them new meaning or a new orientation toward the future? Their writing does reflect movement, and for some an awareness that new orientation is possible. I provide here three examples.

Derek's harsh story "It Could Have Been Me" reveals a horrendous childhood experience. In a discussion of the psalms of lament, a woman once asked me why some of the psalms, such as Psalm 88, don't seem to have any redeeming elements. "They are just dark and painful," she said, pausing, and then adding the answer to her own question. "Sometimes that's all we can do, just cry to God out of the pain." That's what Derek does here. He takes a first tentative step out of suffering by crying out of the depths; he risks telling this story and allowing others to hear it. In "The Perfect Life," Jim's fictional and former troublemaking character Caleb is attempting, with the help of supportive parents, to change his life. Jim shows us that through the metaphor of rebuilding a car. Jesse's "Paradise" offers an awareness that movement out of addiction is desirable. He began revising this poem from much darker earlier drafts during the session in which we discussed Psalm 102 and he made the comments about communication through prayer.

From "It Could Have Been Me"
When I was eleven years old I was living with my biological dad, and he asked me to go to the store. I told him that I didn't want to go and put up a big fight, and he ended up asking my uncle if he would go. My cousin got up and said she wanted to go too. . . . A couple of seconds after they left the house I heard seven gunshots. It scared the crap out of me, and I dropped to the floor. . . . My dad grabbed me and told me that it was my fault. . . . When the cops and all that 'good stuff' got there, they came in and told my dad that they were both dead.

I ran to my room and started replaying the whole goddam thing in my head, and I realized why my dad said it was my fault. It was because if I would have gone to the store, then my uncle and cousin would still be alive. I started to agree with him, and I got up and started throwing things and punching things. Something that was going through my head the whole time was why couldn't it have been me instead? To this day I still wish it were me instead. I don't remember much after that because I just kinda shut down to the world. It wasn't 'til I was fifteen that I asked my dad where my cousin got shot, and when he told me that she got shot once in the right temple and once in the throat I flipped out and started doing some stupid things and didn't care about anyone, and now I'm locked up.

From "The Perfect Life"

See, Caleb used to be a troublemaker. He would get into fights at school, which he had started doing in the sixth grade when he got into a fight with a kid named Dan just because the kid didn't like one of his friends. When he got into high school, he started using drugs and ditching school and football practice just so he could get high or hang out and maybe "get lucky" with some of the girls he was hanging out with. He would be left home alone and go into his parents' bedroom and steal money so that he could get high. . . .

Caleb could always tell the difference between fresh eggs and eggs a couple of days old or bought from the store, just by the sound of the sizzle the eggs made as the bacon grease and egg white cooked together in the frying pan. Were it not for the smell of the cooked food and the coffee, he might have slept until noon. . . .

Caleb finally made his way to his dad. When he asked his dad what was up, his dad pulled off the tarp and presented the 350 Chevrolet V8 big block engine to Caleb. "Wow," exclaimed Caleb as he examined the motor with great admiration. "What are you gonna put it in?"

"Well, I planned on giving it to a special son of mine. . . ." Caleb was finally able to spit out the words, "Thanks, Dad," and gave a smile that shone like the bright evening sun.

From "Paradise"

I'm seeking paradise
Whether in a bottle,
Or formed into a line. . . .
I need to maintain
My frame of mind,
And work to change.
All I need is some answers
In a world where every season it rains.
To answer my questions
I turn to my best friend black tar.
I can imagine my own paradise
But it seems so far.
Will I ever get there?
All I can do is hope and pray
Instead of filling my body
With a different answer every day.

A priest who has worked for many years with adult females in prison said that she hears a common theme from the women she serves: "We know we are guilty, and we are not denying that. What we can't understand is why our family and friends reject us as people. They are unable or unwilling *to separate what we did from who we are.* As a person, I don't exist to them." What I am learning from my students in this ongoing hospice program is that the role of the pastoral caregiver to those who are incarcerated is largely to serve as an antidote to that feeling of despair. It is a ministry of affirming the human being inside of the crew cut, khaki pants, polo shirt, or the yellow cotton set. Prison chaplain Stephen T. Hall emphasizes in ministry with prisoners that no act we have committed can define us or provide the final word about us. "I encourage prisoners to see themselves as God sees them—infinitely valued and unconditionally loved" (171). My students themselves have gracefully articulated how the psalms of disorientation can contribute to that ministry:

"I mean, like saying a prayer when things are hard is a way of communicating when no other communication is possible, and that's what it's like in here."

"This one's saying don't get down on yourself."

"We're all going to die, so do something useful."

"Like now. We need to do it now."

PART THREE
Personal Prayer Life

ॐ

CHAPTER SIX

Let My Prayer Enter Into Your Presence
Praying with the Psalms

Psalms have shaped the private and communal prayers of Jews and Christians for hundreds of years. Jonathan Magonet, author of *A Rabbi Reads the Psalms*, admits that he was not fond of the psalms when he first began to read them because they all sounded alike—in language, terminology, repetition of themes and sentiments. His transformation came when he began translating psalms for a prayer book, and in that process he began to enter the inner world of the psalmists and find ways of linking their world with our own personal history and experience. He recommends taking time with each psalm, living with it, letting "it mature so that it can always be rediscovered afresh." The psalms, Magonet writes, "have nourished and sustained communities and individuals on their own spiritual and life's journeys for over two thousand years, so each reader is challenged to go ever more deeper into them" (2–3, 11–12).

The first five chapters of this book have encouraged more fully integrating psalms of disorientation into worship and pastoral care settings. This chapter considers the importance of these psalms in our private devotions. Although it may seem something of a contradiction to want to go deeper into feelings of sadness, anger, guilt, and alienation, Magonet suggests that the psalms allow us to dwell in these places with God, to cry out of the pain, and that a psalm, each time we encounter it, lends a fresh perspective. As discussed in previous chapters, the psalms can also lead us to a new direction and orientation.

In a similar vein, psalms scholar Claus Westermann writes that the psalms are "inexhaustible." He points out that the two basic sounds accompanying God's actions through history are praise and lament, the polarity of the psalms. The psalmists offer "an immediacy or directness of speaking to God which connects reality in all of its vast extent, depth, and harshness with the God who is the God of both the righteous and the wicked, the God of the depths and the heights, the Lord of creation and the Lord of history" (11–12). Not only do the psalmists speak to the God of our heights, depths, and times in between, but they do so not in prose theological essays, but in lyric poetry, relaying to us their theological insights about God, ourselves, and others, through vivid and imaginative imagery. As C. S. Lewis writes in *Reflections on the Psalms*, the language of poetry in the psalms enables us to make emotional rather than logical connections (10). It is the difference between praying to God, "I think I have a problem and may need some help," and praying to God, "Out of the depths I cry to you, O Lord. Lord, hear my voice! Let your ears be attentive to the voice of my supplications!" (Ps. 130:1–2). We may use our minds in prayer, but emotions open our hearts to God.

The psalms also nurture those of us who long for a world of justice and peace. Dorothy Day devoted her life to helping the hungry, homeless, and other victims of poverty. Cofounder in 1933 of the Catholic Worker, a Roman Catholic movement supporting social justice and pacifism, she believed that feeding the soul was just as important as feeding the body. Day wrote in her autobiography, *The Long Loneliness,* of the deep solace she received from the psalms. "My heart swelled with joy and thankfulness for the Psalms." Those who sang these songs "knew sorrow and expected joy." She said of Psalm 126, "They that sow in tears shall reap in joy. Going, they went and wept, casting their seeds. But coming, they shall come with joyfulness, carrying their sheaves." "If we had faith in what we were doing, making our protest against brutality and injustice, then we were indeed casting our seeds, and there was the promise of the harvest to come" (80–81). The psalmists make abundantly evident their belief in God's support and compassion for the poor and outcast, as the following excerpts show:

> The Lord is a stronghold for the oppressed. . . . For the needy shall not always
>   be forgotten, nor the hope of the poor perish forever. (9:9, 18).
> The helpless commit themselves to you; you have been the helper of the
>   orphan. (10:18)
> God gives the desolate a home to live in; he leads out the prisoners to prosper-
>   ity. (68:6)
> For God delivers the needy when they call, the poor and those who have no
>   helper. God has pity on the weak and needy, and saves the lives of the
>   needy. (72:12–13)
> Let the groans of the prisoners come before you; according to your great
>   power preserve those doomed to die. (79:11)
> God will regard the prayer of the destitute. (102:17)
> God raises up the needy out of distress, and makes their families like flocks
>   (107:41)
> [God] who executes justice for the oppressed; who gives food to the hungry.
>   The Lord sets the prisoners free; the Lord opens the eyes of the blind.
>   The Lord lifts up those who are bowed down. (146:7–8)

Write It, Speak It, Shout It, or Rattle It

Many spiritual directors recommend the psalms as a resource for prayer, and Sr. Mary is one who finds the "difficult" psalms especially appropriate for persons who come to her for directions when they are grieving or when they are in spiritual desolation from other causes. Those in difficult situations are led to know that there is hope after the suffering. Sr. Mary believes the psalms offer those who are suffering a way of praying through their darkness, with the knowledge that others have permitted themselves to wail and grieve to God. In this way, they can give themselves similar permission. In group sessions, she has encouraged participants to write their own psalms and reports that the experience works well once "the timidity at doing so fades." Jacob, another spiritual director, recommends the psalms of sorrow to people who are grieving a serious loss—the death of loved ones but many other kinds of losses as well, such as relationships, financial security, health, and animal companions. One of the men who came to him after the death of his wife found the psalms so beneficial that he began by writing responses to them and then went on to write an entire series of laments. Jacob also suggests memorizing psalms and portions of psalms so that they can be carried in one's heart and drawn upon in moments and periods of difficulty.

Beverly usually begins the process of spiritual direction by asking the person with whom she is working to write a spiritual autobiography, detailing both graces and sorrows. People need to express their feelings about their lives—what has been done to them and what they themselves have done that still troubles them. The psalms of lament can help us express these human emotions that are often so difficult and can be used to educate us about the whole range of human emotions that we experience. "Some people are so shut down, they are not aware of all the difficult things we can feel. The psalmists affirm and validate what we are feeling and help make us aware that these feelings are universal." Beverly believes, too, that these psalms help people go deeper and broader into intimacy with God, validating that we can be totally honest with God. "These things I remember, as I pour out my soul" (Ps. 42:4). "Anytime we can be honest, there is greater capacity for intimacy," Beverly says.

Like most spiritual directors, Susan also seeks spiritual guidance herself, and she relies on the psalms in both relationships. A woman who had been coming to her for spiritual direction over many months recently experienced the sudden death of her son in his mid-thirties from a heart attack, and she also lost her sister to cancer. Despite these losses she continued to go everywhere "with a smile on her face." Susan used the psalms to help her understand the importance of letting herself feel both sorrow and anger. "The psalmists feel whatever they are feeling and don't hesitate to let you know about it." Susan realized she needed the same kind of encouragement from the psalms in an extremely difficult professional situation, and she prayed the psalms of anger in order to express her own. One outcome is a special healing service she has started at her church, a service based on Psalm 130: "Out of the depths I cry to you, O Lord. Lord, hear my voice!"

In *Holy Listening,* her book on the art of spiritual direction, Margaret Guenther encourages reading the psalms and points out that while Psalm 23 offers comfort, Psalm 88 might be more realistic for certain moods: "You have laid me in the depths of the Pit, in dark places, and in the abyss." For those who have difficulty acknowledging their own anger, the psalms that express "extravagant vengefulness" are eye-openers (76). In her work with survivors of sexual abuse, she finds that the psalms, such as Psalm 22 ("My God, my God, why have you forsaken me?") are a great source of strength. The psalmist's imprecations come as a surprise to women schooled in niceness, and she encourages them to read and savor the angry parts. "If the Psalmist could urge God to wreak terrible vengeance on his adversaries, the survivor of abuse can permit herself a little anger. She can write it, speak it, or shout it" (137–138).

Daphne, a spiritual director and retreat leader, added a musical dimension to the writing, speaking, and shouting. Using a translation of the psalms that describes Psalm 7 (a personal lament) as a "frenzied musical rant," she decided to try praying it with musical instruments in a small group, all of whom had percussion-type objects—drums, rattles, bells. As she read each stanza, they made a great racket with the instruments for a minute or so, tapering down to silence. Daphne says the musical accompaniment enhanced the power and quality of the psalm: "We were waking up to God!"

The Practice of Prayer

In one of the stories that introduced the book, Jim, a hospital chaplain who regularly prays the Daily Office, says that he was one of those people who always skipped over the "unpleasant psalms" until he had the experience of ministering to Lila, the rape victim who so needed to express her anger and desire for vindication. Praying the psalms that expressed anger and revenge with Lila helped him see the wholeness of the psalms as a source of prayer.

It is that wholeness that is key: this book is certainly not arguing for praying only psalms of sorrow, suffering, rage, and alienation but rather that for all the reasons that have been addressed in the book, these psalms are important to our private devotions along with those that express the more joyful, ordered, and celebratory parts of our lives. We experience the periods described by Brueggemann as orientation, disorientation, and new orientation. Praying the Psalter's entire range of psalms in our private devotions allows us to communicate with God, directly and honestly, wherever we are in our lives of faith. The willingness to acknowledge and express our deepest feelings to God in times of darkness and imbalance helps us move out of isolation so that we do not remain entrenched there, allowing the transforming light to break through the darkness. Praying the psalms, too, is a way of praying not just for ourselves, but for all of humanity; even if we are not suffering or we are not feeling joyful, we are praying for those who are.

Guenther says that the psalms speak to each of us because they express all of our human emotions: noble and ignoble, trusting and doubtful. They are "strong stuff," giving voice to unacceptable feelings of fear, anger, rage, and the desire for destruction. The psalms begin where we are, in our infallibility and self-centeredness, honestly expressing our needs, praises, thanksgivings, and fears. When we let ourselves enter deeply into the psalms—letting them speak to us and live in us—we see ourselves and our world with new eyes (*My Soul* 13–18).

How one goes about praying the psalms—letting them speak to us and live in us—is an individual matter. The book of Psalms is a book of prayer. Although I discuss here some of the practices, including my own, for praying the psalms, the only basic requirement is one or more preferred translations and reading or singing each psalm with an open heart. Some of the translations I use are *The Book of Common Prayer*, the *New Revised Standard Version*, the *King James Version*, *The Inclusive Psalms* (translated by Priests for Equality), and *The Book of Psalms—A New Translation According to the Traditional Hebrew Text* by the Jewish Publication Society. Every translation is an "interpretation," so it can be interesting and insightful to look at more than one.

A traditional way praying the psalms and other scripture that has been used for many centuries is *lectio divina* (sacred reading). Developed by monastics in the early and medieval church, this process involves (1) reading the psalm slowly and reverentially, listening deeply; (2) meditating on the passage, allowing it to connect to experiences and memories, to stir the imagination, following the text wherever it leads; (3) praying, having a conversation with God out of the meditation; and (4) finishing by simply resting in God's presence. The intent of *lectio* remains, as it has through the centuries, is spending time with God in a manner that deepens the experience of God's presence.

Old Testament scholar Toni Craven writes in *The Book of Psalms* that the psalms teach us that prayer changes things, and all of our life experience must be brought before God. Paralleling Brueggemann's psalms of new orientation, she suggests that many psalms speak of singing a "new song" to God. Any new song for us is born of our lived experiences, and prayer becomes new when our hearts are open to the gift of God's love. The wide variety of expressions in the psalms show us we need not fear speaking in a language that reflects the totality of what it means to be human. The "new song" becomes increasingly possible as we grow in familiarity with the psalms by taking time with them. Her process of praying the psalms includes keeping a journal with reflections, such as (1) imagining who the author of the psalm is, who could have said the kind of words that are in the psalm, and what kind of life experience might have occasioned the writing of the psalm; (2) noting the poetic patterns (such as images) that organize the psalm; beliefs, attitudes, or values that are striking; and positive and negative features that attract or repel; (3) looking at commentaries to see what scholars have found in the psalm; and (4) taking time to write a prayer or one's feelings about the psalms. Craven points out that the mysterious trust pervading the psalms is that God holds out a future of hope. What matters most to the psalmists is not saying a particular set of "right" words to or about God but maintaining a dynamic relationship with God (11, 147–148).

A Personal Journey with the Psalms

For a number of years, as part of my morning quiet time, I have prayed the psalms using as a Scripture guide the Daily Office Lectionary from *The Book of Common Prayer* (934–1001), which arranges readings from Scripture for a two-year period, with the psalms appointed in a seven-week cycle. Following this kind of daily lectionary, and there are many available, ensures coverage of all the psalms several times a year, within a context of other readings from the Old Testament and New Testament. My own prayer life goes through cycles, and what does not speak to me in one cycle may connect strongly in another. After reading the psalm or psalms appointed in the daily lectionary, I consider what stands out on a given day—some particular verse or image, several lines or phrases, a story in the poem, or the overall theme of the psalm. Frequently, questions come up that help me draw meaning from the psalm and lead to spiritual connection with something ongoing in my life and community. The starting point for responding to a psalm is usually one of the following:
• An image will trigger a memory or an awareness—from childhood or a decade ago or the previous day. It may be a person, an action, a feeling, or an experience, but the image connects with something that has spiritual content that I want to explore.

- A particular theme will emerge from the psalm and generate ideas, such as a psalm about darkness and light coexisting, anger, shame, fear of death, nations in turmoil, grief, people treating each other unkindly, or God as our source of strength and comfort.
- I bring something to the process—such as a difficult question, an emotional struggle, a political issue or other current story in the news—and there will be something in the psalm that speaks to that circumstance.

I then spend a few moments in silent reflection and prayer. On many mornings, I add a step to the process by taking time to write a short response— usually just a few sentences—to the psalm and my day's experience with it. I find that the act of writing adds a less controlled and more creative dimension to my reflection, but not through rewriting the psalm. It is a creative response to the psalmist's personal experience and expression of spirituality. Often, a new idea or insight emerges from the writing that hadn't occurred to me in the silent reflection on the psalm. Over the years that I've written reflections—including many from periods of struggle, sorrow, and difficulty—the psalmists have offered an ongoing expression of God's presence, even if I am feeling alienated, and a vision of God who supports and loves me. Going through the Daily Office cycle, it is interesting and revealing to see how different my own responses are to the same psalms, the same verses, and the same images—each time they appear. The writing allows for interaction with the poetic language, images, and rhythm of the psalm as well as the poet's experience, in a way that is unencumbered by my analytical mind and inner critic. The writing may lead to new understanding, but sometimes just acknowledging the situation and communicating that to God is helpful.

Over the years that I have followed this daily practice, I have written hundreds of reflections on psalms, and this "psalm journal" documents my personal seasons of orientation, disorientation, and new orientation. Much in the writing is delightful and celebratory, but many, many reflections deal with suffering and anguish for me and for those to whom I am closely connected. Having the written responses enables me to go back and read about my own process through challenging and sorrowful times. Sometimes reading about them stirs up the same feelings I had with the original experience. The reflections on losses remind me, for example, that my grieving does not end. As I get older, my losses accumulate, and I grieve more and more the people and places and things that are gone forever as a presence in my daily life. But I also read in these passages the healing and transformation that occurs. As the psalmists experience a living God across the range of human emotions, including extremely unpleasant ones, so do I. Guenther (cited above) suggests letting the psalms live in us, and my psalm journal is one of the ways I do that.

As I went through some of my psalm reflections in preparation for writing this chapter, I found a seed of the book in a response written many, many years ago, long before I knew of Brueggemann's work and the classification of "psalms of disorientation." In response to Psalm 88:2 (BCP)—"Let my prayer enter into your presence; incline your ear to my lamentation"— I wrote the following:

> In my study group this week, some of the participants were talking about how "complaining" and "woe is me" the psalmists are. Certainly Psalm 88 is one that is filled with whining and woe. The psalmist writes of lamentation, trouble, having no strength, being laid in the depths of the pit, being abandoned by friends, feeling rejected and wretched. My reaction to these psalms has always been different. I appreciate that I can come before God with these honest feelings. I don't have them all of the time, but I do have them some of the time. The psalmists prays—pleas—for God's help, acknowledging the need for God during these hard periods.

Responding to Psalms of Disorientation: Three Examples

To illustrate this way of praying the psalms, I will use three psalms from the Daily Office for a day when all of the appointed psalms for morning and evening are psalms of disorientation:* Psalm 80, Psalm 77, and Psalm 79. The following demonstrates the approaches—image, theme, bringing a topic—and includes some of my responses to these psalms, which are obviously individual to me, but are offered here to show how the response is generated from the image, or theme, or what I bring to the psalm.

Psalm 80
Give ear, O Shepherd of Israel, you who lead Joseph like a flock!
You who are enthroned upon the cherubim, shine forth
before Ephraim and Benjamin and Manasseh.
Stir up your might, and come to save us!
Restore us, O God; let your face shine, that we may be saved.
O Lord God of hosts, how long will you be angry with your people's prayers?
You have fed them with the bread of tears, and given them tears to drink in
    full measure.
You make us the scorn of our neighbors; our enemies laugh among themselves.
Restore us, O God of hosts; let your face shine that we may be saved.
You brought a vine out of Egypt; you drove out the nations and planted it.
You cleared the ground for it; it took deep root and filled the land.
The mountains were covered with its shade, the mighty cedars with its
    branches;
it sent out its branches to the sea, and its shoots to the River.
Why then have you broken down its walls, so that all who pass along the way
    pluck its fruit?
The boar from the forest ravages it, and all that move in the field feed upon it.
Turn again, O God of hosts; look down from heaven, and see; have regard for
    this vine, the stock that your right hand planted.

---

* This particular combination of psalms occurs on Mondays during the 5th week of Epiphany, the 3rd week of Lent, the 6th week of Easter, and four times during the Season after Pentecost.

They have burned it with fire, they have cut it down; may they perish at the rebuke of your countenance.

But let your hand be upon the one at your right hand, the one whom you made strong for yourself.

Then we will never turn back from you; give us life, and we will call on your name.

Restore us, O LORD God of hosts; let your face shine, that we may be saved.

Images: listening ear, shepherd and flock, God enthroned and shining forth, tribal leaders, stirring up power, God's face shining, tears for food and drink, neighbors mocking, enemies laughing, a healthy vine, clearing ground and planting, shaded mountains, mighty cedars, branches growing into the sea, shoots into rivers, broken walls, plucking fruit, ravaging boars, God's stock, God's hand, burning fire, God's name.

Themes: God's shepherding through history; the paradox of God being both present and absent; repetition of the prayer for restoration, salvation, and God's face to shine; God's anger; God's people feeling alienated; being badly treated both by neighbors and enemies; need for feeding by God; God's fruitful planting gone amok; plea for God to nurture what God planted; vow of faithfulness to God; the benediction used in worship services of Christians and Jews, "The Lord make his face to shine upon you, and be gracious to you."

Some subjects I have brought to this psalm for reflection: lack of progress in Middle East peace process; discussion about America's image with a friend who traveled to Egypt to visit in-laws; our need for tears in grief; faces shining in the transfiguration; mountaintop experiences and our lives mostly lived in the valley; sense of alienation from God.

Response 1

The paradox in this psalm of God being here (a shepherd leading the flock) and not here (God's face not shining forth) led to a response during a period when I felt that my church community was alienated from one another as well as from God because of internal strife and dissension. What I noticed in the psalm is that the people clearly feel abandoned by God, but they wait in full confidence of God's presence. While they wait, they lament because they have not been fed properly—they've been fed tears—and because what God has given them is in a big mess; while they wait, they also pray, which is an act of faith. The psalm reminds me that Advent is always with us in the sense of expectation. Where there is disorder and brokenness, as is the situation in the psalm, the expectation is for God's face to shine. We talk to God expectantly, as I am doing in my morning meditation, even while God is absent.

Response 2

When my daughter was at the rebellious worst of her teenage years and I had serious doubts about her future, I wrote on this psalm's theme of "nurturing our plantings." Across the back of my property, the previous owners had planted a row of shrubs. Some produced a beautiful green leaf tinted with copper, and some had no foliage at all. On the advice of gardening friends, I watered the unhealthy ones profusely, but that didn't help. Nothing else, such as putting mulch around them, helped either. The healthy plants continued to thrive, and the unhealthy ones to wither. One afternoon in a fit of anger at my daughter's behavior, I marched out to the toolshed and selected the largest clippers in the shed. I hacked and whacked off all the dead growth, every brown leaf and every drooping branch until all that was left of the unhealthy shrubs were stumps and leafless branches. In the process, I hacked and whacked off all the anger at my daughter. Several days later, I noticed new growth emerging from the withered stumps.

I would like to add as a postscript that, fourteen years later, daughter and plants are thriving.

Psalm 77
I cry aloud to God, aloud to God, that he may hear me.
In the day of my trouble I seek the Lord; in the night my hand is stretched out
    without wearying; my soul refuses to be comforted.
I think of God, and I moan; I meditate, and my spirit faints.
You keep my eyelids from closing; I am so troubled that I cannot speak.
I consider the days of old, and remember the years of long ago.
I commune with my heart in the night; I meditate and search my spirit;
"Will the Lord spurn forever, and never again be favorable?
Has his steadfast love ceased forever? Are his promises at an end for all time?
Has God forgotten to be gracious? Has he in anger shut up his compassion?"
And I say, "It is my grief that the right hand of the Most High has changed."
I will call to mind the deeds of the LORD; I will remember your wonders of old.
I will meditate on all your work, and muse on your mighty deeds.
Your way, O God, is holy. What god is so great as our God?
You are the God who works wonders; you have displayed your might among
    the peoples.
With your strong arm you redeemed your people, the descendants of Jacob
    and Joseph.
When the waters saw you, O God, when the waters saw you, they were
    afraid; the very deep trembled.
The clouds poured out water; the skies thundered; your arrows flashed on
    every side.
The crash of your thunder was in the whirlwind; your lightnings lit up the
    world; the earth trembled and shook.
Your way was through the sea, your path, through the mighty waters; yet
    your footprints were unseen.
You led your people like a flock by the hand of Moses and Aaron.

Images: crying to God, night, outstretched hand, comfortless soul, moaning, meditating, fainting spirit, open eyelids, olden days, God's spurning and anger, grief, God's right hand, God's wonders of old, God's strong arm, descendants of Jacob and Joseph, waters that are afraid and trembling, clouds raining, skies thundering, flashing arrows, whirlwind, lightning, trembling earth, path through mighty waters, footprints unseen, God as shepherd.

Themes: Crying out to God from desperate situations and how we feel when we are suffering; personal grief; remembering God's love and covenant; God's capacity to transform, even our grief; God's working wonders; God's power to redeem; evidence of God's work even though God's footprints are unseen.

Subjects I have brought to this psalm for reflection: tsunami disaster in Asia; earthquake near my daughter's home in California; issues in bereavement support group; dealing with night wakefulness; philosopher Charles Hartshorne's death; getting caught in a mountain thunderstorm; a friend's volunteer work for the Red Cross, traveling across the country to help with flood relief.

Reflection 1

In chapter 3, I discussed some of the ways I have integrated the psalms of sorrow into my work with hospice bereavement support groups. Psalms such as this one suggested the connection because it is a personal cry to God from one who is grieving. What I wrote in a reflection on this psalm was about my own grief. Much in this psalm is descriptive of persons who are grieving. "I cry aloud, my soul refuses to be comforted, I moan, my spirit faints, I cannot sleep, I remember the days of old, I chew over things in the night, I feel spurned by God." Although grieving is a distinct journey for each individual, there are common elements, and those described by the psalmists are some of them. As much as I've learned from my work with hospice, none of it helped me deal with the anger I felt when my own mother died after suffering a long, debilitating illness, losing her mental capacity well ahead of her physical body; nothing helped, that is, except to recognize that I needed help and support myself in my grief. There were many days when, like the psalmist, my soul refusing to be comforted, and all I could do was cry out.

Reflection 2

The tsunami tragedy in Asia was on my mind as I read this psalm's verses about waters that are afraid and trembling, the seeming opposite of tsunami waves. News accounts reported the enormous loss of life; the elimination of entire families; the damage to homes and property; the impact on individuals, families, and communities; and vivid images of those who were suffering in the aftermath of the waves that overwhelmed. I asked the question raised by the psalmist, "Has God forgotten to be gracious?" The answer came from the psalm itself, that the God of this psalm is the God for all times, the God through all of history, the God whose way is holy.

What that means* in confronting a communal tragedy of this magnitude as well as for our individual losses is that those whom we *lose* are *not lost* because they are not lost to God: they are forever a part of God's realm. [Author's note: Since I wrote this reflection, Hurricane Katrina has devastated the Gulf Coast. This psalm also seems an especially appropriate prayer for that tragedy.]

Psalm 79
O God, the nations have come into your inheritance; they have defiled your
   holy temple; they have laid
Jerusalem in ruins.
They have given the bodies of your servants to the birds of the air for food,
   the flesh of your faithful to the wild animals of the earth.
They have poured out their blood like water all around Jerusalem, and there
   was no one to bury them.
We have become a taunt to our neighbors, mocked and derided by those
   around us.
How long, O LORD? Will you be angry forever? Will your jealous wrath burn
   like fire?
Pour out your anger on the nations that do not know you, and on the king-
   doms that do not call your name.
For they have devoured Jacob and laid waste his habitation.
Do not remember against us the iniquities of our ancestors; let your compassion come speedily to meet us,
for we are brought very low.
Help us, O God of our salvation, for the glory of your name; deliver us, and
   forgive our sins, for your name's sake.
Why should the nations say, "Where is their God?" Let the avenging of the
   outpoured blood of your servants be known among the nations before
   our eyes.
Let the groans of the prisoners come before you; according to your great
   power preserve those doomed to die.
Return sevenfold into the bosom of our neighbors the taunts with which they
   taunted you, O LORD!
Then we your people, the flock of your pasture, will give thanks to you forever;
   from generation to generation we will recount your praise.

Images: holy temples defiled, Jerusalem in ruins, servant's bodies given for food, birds of the air, wild animals, blood pouring like water, unburied corpses, neighbors mocking and taunting, God's anger and jealousy, sins of our ancestors, God's compassion meeting us, groans of prisoners, returning taunts sevenfold, God's people as flock.
Themes: situation beyond human repair; prayer for God's intervention in disastrous situation; need for God's compassion; communal feeling that core is disintegrating, revealed through grotesque images; requests for vindication; vision of God as double-sided: vengeful and compassionate;

---

* This idea was suggested in a sermon at St. James Episcopal Church, Austin, Texas, preached by the Rev. W. S. Adams.

anger as common emotion in disorientation; struggle is ongoing, but vision of new orientation in psalm's ending.

Subjects I have brought to this psalm for reflection: 9/11, wars in Iraq and Afghanistan; recurring violence in the Middle East; deaths and injuries during election in Iraq; homeless problem in my city; proposed federal budget cuts affecting disadvantaged; my students at the Youth Detention Center; Flannery O'Connor's fiction.

Refection 1

Meditating on Psalm 79 helped me gain some insight into my work teaching incarcerated youth and my expectations about it. When I began teaching creative writing to imprisoned teenagers, I had a grand vision—affirmed by their enormous intelligence, talent, and energy—that their lives would make a dramatic turn for the better as a result of our process together, and they would go on to productive lives on the outside. Several have been released to work and halfway programs, but so far all but one have violated parole and returned to incarceration. I was especially disappointed when Raul came back. He was so capable and so eager to be out. Raul wrote about the experience of being free for a moment in time: "I found one thing that I'm sad to say I've almost forgotten about behind these walls and locked doors. And that's beauty. Just the sound of the word should be enough to keep a person out of trouble." But it didn't. How could he write that and get into trouble again, almost immediately? The difficulty of change reflects how deeply rooted and complex the students' problems are. "Let the groans of the prisoners come before you" (Ps. 79:11). I am leaning from my students that the class, like the Psalter, is a place for expressing emotions honestly and for freeing the imagination.

Reflection 2

The prayer in this psalm is a plea for God's intervention in a situation that is beyond human repair, which is how I felt following the terrorist attacks of 9/11 and again when the United States responded. We responded to violence with more violence. To those who say they avoid some psalms because the psalmists promote violence, I would say the opposite, that this shows the grotesque results of violence. The corpses are lying around to be fed upon. God's people have been bloodied and left as food for the birds and wild beasts. Those who remain are reviled. In the midst of the decay and an eroding core comes the psalmist's soulful yearning for God: "Help us, O God of our salvation." In a circumstance of acute national disorientation, the psalmist appeals to God, affirming trust in God's salvation and compassion. It is a plea on behalf of a nation's soul, and in a larger sense the soul of nations universal.

What We Find and What We Bring

Those who regularly pray the psalms generally find their own rhythm and style, I hope that the ideas presented in the chapter are helpful in developing or building on one's own process of prayer. In his book *Praying the Psalms*, Brueggemann suggests that praying the psalms depends on two things: what we find when we come to the psalms that is already there and what we bring to the psalms from our own lives. What we find is eloquence, passion, and boldness in addressing the Holy One. What we should bring to the psalms as we pray is a candid openness to the extremities in our own lives and in the lives of our companions. The extremities recognize the depths of despair and death, and acknowledge the sheer gift of life. "The work of prayer is to bring these two realities together . . . in order that we may be addressed by a Word that outdistances all our speech" (27).

The experiences with the psalms that people have been willing to share for this book strongly affirm Brueggemann's idea about the work of prayer and its mystery. The story that flows from the psalms does not end either with our own words or with those of the psalmists. There is something infinitely greater in our praying the psalms than what is already there, in the texts, or in what we bring to them.

ॐ

A Psalms Workshop

Psalms for a Time of Trouble: The "Difficult" Psalms in Worship, Prayer, and Pastoral Care

Audiences and Settings:

Pastoral caregivers and chaplains (hospital, nursing home, hospice, prison); youth ministers; clergy conferences; adult education classes; Scripture study groups; prayer/support groups; parish retreats

Materials Needed for Each Participant:

Bible

Lyn Fraser, *Prayers from the Darkness: The Difficult Psalms*

Handouts if needed (page references to the book indicate material appropriate for using as workshop handouts or PowerPoint presentations).

To the Leader:

In making presentations to the kinds of groups for which the workshops are designed, I have found that this common body of information—some background on the wholeness of the psalms as a source of prayer, explanation of how the "difficult" psalms reflect our life process, and discussion of how these psalms offer the potential for transformation and healing— provides an essential context for the examples and activities selected to fit a workshop's particular focus. The psalm examples in *Prayers from the Darkness* provide additional illustrations, and suggestions for discussions to supplement those are provided in the workshop outline.

These workshops are planned for a half-day, three to four hours, but the time can be extended or reduced through the choice of examples and activities. Workshops can also be modified for presentation to specific groups; for example, if the participants in a pastoral caregivers' workshop primarily minister to the terminally ill and bereaved, examples can be selected to fit that audience, and the workshop leader can draw on additional discussion from relevant sections of the book.

The following table, "Psalm References in Book," is provided as a resource for workshop leaders. (Note that numbers in the table refer to psalms, not page numbers in the book.)

Psalm References In Book

Situation, Theme, or Topic	Psalm(s)
Introduction	
Hospice patient angry at God	68, 79
Rape victim: how to pray against attacker	58, 59
Veteran battling addiction: spent, crushed; shame, guilt	38
Church community in disarray; need for reconciliation	120
New church member: range of feelings that are "fair" to pray	55
Grieving widow: sleeplessness, stress, mistreatment	4
Church educator treated unjustly; need to express vengeance	109
Parish community post 9/11: who are the righteous & wicked?	37
Chapter One	
Examples of psalms not prayed on Sundays	
Desire for vindication	35
Violation of sacred spaces	74
Mistreatment by friends	88
Acute isolation	102
Mortality	39
Examples of psalms prayed on Sundays	16, 34, 104, 138
Example: Psalm of Orientation	8
Psalm of Disorientation	6
Psalm of New Orientation	30
Psalms appointed but with verses omitted	25, 85, 71
Communal lament appropriate to post 9/11	74
Movement within psalms at beginning of chapter	35, 74, 88, 102, 39
Importance of praying the psalms in community	86
Chapter Two	
Psalms with optional omissions in Daily Office Lectionary	63, 110, 137
Psalms not prayed on Sundays: what we miss	44, 64
Structure of laments	64
Preaching the psalms	
Acknowledging anger; moving congregation towards forgiveness	58
John Donne sermon on death	89
Dietrich Bonhoeffer sermon on vengeance	58
Images in the psalms	42
Following psalm's movement	3
Expressing and healing anger	52
Bringing a situation to the psalm	58, 37

I. Introduction

Ask participants to introduce themselves and say something about why they are attending the workshop session.

Introduce yourself and your own area of interest regarding the topic.

II. Background

The psalms originated more than two thousand years ago, probably between 1300 and 500 B.C.E., and were passed down orally for many years before being recorded in written form. They remain an incomparable spiritual resource in part because the psalmists express the same emotions that we experience in the twenty-first century. They cover a wide range—conveying joy, praise, thanksgiving, and delight in God's creation and order and goodness. But they also express feelings that relate to our times of struggle, suffering, and turmoil, such as grief, guilt, anger, envy, disappointment, revenge, and alienation.

Almost 40 percent of the psalms in the book of Psalms are about individuals and communities in periods of distress and difficulty, and those psalms are the topic of this workshop. (**See p. 26, "Psalms of Disorientation."**)

Churches tend to avoid these psalms in the lectionaries we follow for worship because they deal with things that are not pleasant to hear and say and sing. For the same reasons many individuals also avoid these psalms.

The words of these psalms, however, reflect where we are at times in our lives, as individuals, but also in community: grieving the loss of a loved one or the loss of a job or a home or a pet or a family from divorce; serious illness; aging; trauma; addiction; and communal groups, churches, workplaces, the nation, and our world in disharmony and disarray. The purpose of the book and this workshop is to encourage more widespread use of these psalms in worship, pastoral care, and in private prayer because they help us and help others move through these periods of disorientation to a place of healing and balance.

Those who wrote the psalms admit their feelings directly and honestly, ask for God's help, and then express faith and trust in God's response. This is not to suggest that the psalms provide instant healing, but they can contribute in a transforming way to the healing process.

III. Psalms and Life Process

These difficult psalms are an outgrowth of categories developed by Old Testament scholar Walter Brueggemann.

Our lives are not static, and the psalms classifications that Brueggemann developed reflect our life process. We move from seasons when things are going well in our lives, seasons of **orientation;** to periods of anguish and disarray and alienation, times of **disorientation;** to **new orientation,** where light breaks through the darkness, and we regain balance and energy.

Point out examples of each kind of psalm. **(See pp. 23-24, "Examples: Psalms of Orientation [Psalm 8], Disorientation [Psalm 6], and New Orientation [Psalm 30].)**

Grieving is an example of this process. When we experience a major loss, we move from relative orientation to disorientation, which may be severe depending on the nature of the loss. Grieving helps us move to new orientation, where we are able to reinvest energy in living. We continue to grieve, but the grief no longer dominates our lives. We are also never the same because grief changes us. We sing to the Lord a new song.

In this workshop we focus on the psalms of disorientation, which acknowledge our periods of despair and suffering. These psalms help us move toward new orientation by expressing the pain and asking God for help and showing us that God hears us in our time of need.

IV. Examples

Depending on the audience for your workshop, provide several stories of situations in which these psalms have been helpful. **(See pp. 11-17, for stories of individuals and communities helped by difficult psalms.)**

See also chapters in the book on using these psalms in pastoral care ministry to the terminally ill and bereaved (**Chapter 3**); those suffering from illness, aging, and other losses such as divorce and unemployment (**Chapter 4**); and teens, including youth who are incarcerated (**Chapter 5**).

To incorporate the difficult psalms into worship through sermons and special services, including a service of lament, see (**Chapter 2**).

To use these psalms in our private devotions, see (**Chapter 6**).

Finally, ask participants to offer any stories from their own pastoral care experiences with psalms of trouble and sorrow, as well as responses to any of the examples you have shared.

V. How These Psalms Help

1. Movement

The difficult psalms, which are psalms of lament, move from anguish and pain to hope and relief. The psalmists describe a situation but provide evidence that God hears their prayers. Something changes in the psalms; we usually do not know what has happened to effect the change, but we can see the transformation.

There are several ways to illustrate this movement. One is to discuss the structure of lament psalms. **(See pp. 36–37; 68–69, for a discussion of the structure of lament psalms.)**

Although laments have different details and situations, they follow a form that includes a plea to God (addressing God intimately, stating what is wrong and requests for God's actions; sometimes imprecations against those causing the problems, motivations for God to act, such as flattering God or showing the innocence of the speaker or reminding God of past deeds), and a doxology (assurance of God's hearing our prayers; praise and thanksgiving).

Turn to Psalm 3 in your Bible.

Discuss the sections of the psalm.

Intimate address: Lord, O Lord

Description of problem/complaint: How many adversaries I have, How many rise up against me. They say, "There is no help in God." (Enemies may be illnesses, harsh words.)

Actions needed: Rise up and set me free.

Sometimes the request for vindication: Strike the enemies across the face, break their teeth. (Shows how bad things are.)

Motivations for God to act: You are a shield, a glory, the one who lifts my head.

Evidence of being heard: I call aloud and God answers me. I lie down and sleep, I wake again because the Lord sustains me; I do not fear.

Doxology: Deliverance belongs to the Lord, your blessing be upon your people.

Compare the psalmist's situation in verses 1 and 2 to 5 and 6.

> How many are my foes! Many are rising against me; many are saying to me, "There is no help for you in God." (vv. 1–2)
> I lie down and sleep; I wake again, for the Lord sustains me. I am not afraid of ten thousands of people who have set themselves against me all around. (vv. 5–6)

Another way to show the movement, is to look at the complaints and expressions of faith in psalms of lament.

These psalms help us move by expressing the pain, asking God for help, and showing that God hears us in our time of need. All of the psalms of lament follow this form in various ways with different details and situations, but they all move in this way to God.

(**Psalm 88** offers another model for prayer, where there is no movement. Unlike most laments, the psalmist's plea in Psalm 88 goes unanswered. There are times when the only authentic communication with God is the bluntly honest admission of feeling abandoned and left in a grim place. At the same time, the psalmist's prayer—God of my salvation, let my prayer come before you, incline your ear to my cry—is an act of trust in God.)

2. Conversation Patterns in the Psalms

Another way the psalms are helpful is by reflecting how we express ourselves when we are suffering—for example, by repeating ourselves again and again.

A characteristic of Hebrew poetry is a rhythmic pattern of repetition called parallelism. (**See pp. 73–74 for examples of parallelism**.) Short phrases or entire verses may be parallel to one another.

Three common types of parallelism are to repeat what has been said before in a slightly different way, to contrast a positive statement with a negative statement, and to add or develop the original idea.

Show an example with **Psalm 102**.

Saying what has been said before in a slightly different way.
Hear my prayer, let my cry come to you. (v. 1)

Contrasting positive with negative statement.
Do not hide your face from me; incline your ear to me. (v. 2)

Adding on to or developing an idea
My bones burn like a furnace; my bones cling to my skin. (vv. 3, 5)
I am like and owl in the wilderness, like a little owl of the waste places, like a lonely bird on a housetop. (vv. 6–7)

Then relate these conversation patterns to how we speak to God and others when we are hurting: saying the same thing again and again, in different ways; saying something in contrasting ways, like an internal argument; building and embellishing the story, adding layers that sometimes help reveal what is most important or to be more convincing about how hard things are for us.

One of the benefits is that these patterns in the psalms affirm the natural rhythms of the person who is speaking and the need to go over the same ground again and again. Another benefit is the way in which these common patterns of speaking convey empathy with the psalmist speaking in the same manner that we do.

VI. Activities

Depending on the amount of time available for the workshop as well as the composition of participants and their objectives, choose from the following activities.

1. **Select eight to twelve difficult psalms** (e.g., 6, 13, 22, 26, 31, 32, 35, 55, 64, 74, 70, 80, 120, 126, 130, 137, 140).

Working in small groups, ask participants to identify types of situations—as individuals and in communities—in which each psalm might be helpful and explain why. Have each small group report on its suggestions and discussion to the entire workshop. Another way to do this activity with a small workshop group would be to assign one psalm to each participant, have them develop a response, and then each person would report to the entire group.

2. **Work in pairs (or small groups). Ask the participants to think of a current circumstance in their personal or communal lives that is challenging. Instruct the partner (or others in the group) to find a psalm from among the difficult psalms appropriate to that situation and explain why it is appropriate.**

Have each participant report to the entire group the pastoral situation, recommended psalm, and any relevant discussion and response.

3. **Creative response to the psalms.**

Provide each person with a copy of two psalms from the list of difficult psalms. Give the following directions clearly and quickly: "Without thinking too much, select one of these two psalms. [Allow time.] In the psalm, quickly choose one word or phrase—something that jumps out at you. [Allow time.] Write that word or phrase in the center of the page. [Allow time.]

Write around this word or phrase in a big circle any words or phrases that you associate with the original word. [Allow time, but encourage doing this quickly.] Draw a circle around each new word/phrase. [Allow time.] Draw lines between the words/phrases that are connected in some way. [Allow time.] Look at what you have.

"Without thinking, begin writing—anything you want. Don't worry about grammar, spelling, or punctuation. Just write what comes to you, letting it flow." [Allow five minutes.]

Ask participants if they would like to share from this process, either the word they chose and the associations, the actual writing, or both.

4. Reflective response to the psalms.

Provide each person with two or three difficult psalms and ask them to choose one to work with in this process.

Ask them to circle all the images in the psalm. Then identify one image that grabs them.

Ask them to identify the themes in the psalm, the main ideas.

Ask them to write down something—an issue, a question, a problem, a grace—that is currently important in their personal prayers.

Choose one of these three approaches: image, theme, current prayer topic. Write for five minutes, letting the writing flow freely without worrying about grammar, spelling, and punctuation.

5. Working individually, in pairs, or in small groups, write a psalm of lament, using the lament structure:

Plea
> Intimate address to God
> Description of the problems
> Requests of God
> Motivations for God to act (flattering God, innocence of speaker, reminders of God's past deeds)
> Imprecations (optional)

Praise
> Assurance of being heard
> Praise and thanksgiving

6. This activity can be done by each participant or in small groups. Select one individual lament (e.g., 6, 13, 25, 59) and one communal lament (e.g., 74, 79, 126, 137).

— Identify images in the psalms
— Identify themes in the psalms
— Find the movement through the psalm from anguish to hope
— Discuss how the psalm might be used in
> • a pastoral care situation
> • in a sermon
> • in a service of communal worship

7. Ask each participant to choose a psalm from the list of difficult psalms.

— Imagine who the author is, who could have said the words in the psalm

— Identify how poetic devices such as images are used to organize the psalmist's beliefs, attitudes, and values
— List the features of the psalm that attract or repel you
— Write a prayer or your feelings about the psalm

8. Select a psalm from the list of difficult psalms. Working individually or in small groups, have each participant

— Identify an image in the psalm that triggers a strong reaction or awareness or memory, something that has spiritual content to explore
— Select a theme from the psalm (e.g. guilt, grief, shame, fear of death, nations in turmoil, people treating each other unkindly, God as source of strength in times of trouble)
— Bring something to the psalm such as a challenging situation in your personal or professional life and find something in the psalm that relates to that circumstance.
— Write a brief reflection or prayer on the process using one of these three approaches.

9. Working either with the entire group or in small groups, create a collaborative psalm. One person writes the first verse, passes it to the next person who adds a verse, continuing until everyone has contributed a verse.

10. Hold a service of lament, the form of which is provided at the end of chapter 2.

VII. Conclusion

Summarize what you have done in the workshop.
• Background on the psalms.
• Explanation of how the difficult psalms fit our life process, with concrete examples showing how the psalms have been helpful to individuals and communities.
• Discussion of how the difficult psalms can be helpful in the healing process by propelling movement from anguish and pain to trust and hope—crying out of the painful situations in faith, reflecting conversation patterns of those who are suffering, and conveying empathy.
• Participation in activities to provide practical experience in using the difficult psalms in personal prayer life, pastoral care, and communal worship.

As time permits, ask participants for any questions or comments, including examples of ways in which the workshop met (or did not meet) their expectations.

WORKS CITED

Blumenthal, David R. "Confronting the Character of God." *God in the Fray: Divine Ambivalence in the Hebrew Bible*. Ed. T. Beal and T. Linafelt. Philadelphia: Fortress Press, 1997. 9 Nov. 2004. <http://www.js.emory.edu/BLUMENTHAL/Brueggemann2.html>.

———. "Re: Query: Psalm 44." E-mail to Lyn Fraser. 8 Nov. 2004.

Bonhoeffer, Dietrich. "Sermon on a Psalm of Vengeance," Qtd. in "A Bonhoeffer Sermon." Daniel Bloesch. *Theology Today*. Jan. 1982. 9 Nov. 2004. <http://theologytoday.ptsem.edu/jan1982/v38-4-article3.htm>.

The Book of Common Prayer. New York: Church Publishing Incorporated, 1979.

Brand, E. L. Qtd. in *The Psalms and Other Studies of the Old Testament*, Ed. Jack C. Knight and Lawrence A. Sinclair. Cincinnati: Forward Movement Publications, 1990. 67.

Brueggemann, Walter. *The Message of the Psalms*. Minneapolis: Augsburg Publishing House, 1984.

———. *Praying the Psalms*. Winona, MN: Saint Mary's Press, 1986.

———. "Covenanting as Human Vocation: The Relation of the Bible and Pastoral Care." In *The Psalms and the Life of Faith*. Ed. Patrick D. Miller. Minneapolis: Fortress Press, 1995.

Bryson, Bill. *The Mother Tongue*. New York: W. Morrow, 1990.

Crafton, Barbara Cawthorne. *Meditations on the Psalms*. Harrisburg, PA: Morehouse Publishing, 1996.

Craigie, Peter C. *Word Bible Commentary, Psalms 1–50*. Vol. 19. Waco, TX: Word Books, 1983.

Craven, Toni. *The Book of Psalms*. Collegeville, MN: The Liturgical Press. 1992.

Craven, Toni, and Harrelson, Walter. "The Psalms." *The New Interpreter's Study Bible*. Nashville: Abingdon Press., 2003.

Davis, Ellen F. *Getting Involved with God: Rediscovering the Old Testament*. Cambridge, Mass.: Cowley Publications, 2001.

Day, Dorothy. *The Long Loneliness*. San Francisco: Harper & Row, Publishers, 1952.

Donne, John. "Preached to the L.L. upon Easter Day, at the Communion." *John Donne: Eighty Sermons* 27/Rev. 11 Dec. 1998. 9 Nov. 2004. <http.//www.users.csbsju.edu/~eknuth/jd/easter.html>.

———. "Death, be not proud." *Responding to Literature*. Ed. Judith A. Stanford. 2nd ed. Mountain View, CA: Mayfield Publishing Company, 1996. 1166.

Dunbar, Paul Laurence. "We Wear the Mask." *Responding to Literature*. Ed. Judith A. Stanford. 2nd. ed. Mountain View, CA: Mayfield Publishing Company, 1996. 412.

Episcopal Church. "Revised Common Lectionary." Standing Committee on Liturgy and Music. 2 Dec. 2004. <http://www.episcopalchurch.org/19625_19606_ENG_HTM.htm>.

Frost, Robert. "The Road Not Taken." *Responding to Literature*. Ed. Judith A. Stanford. 2nd ed. Mountain View, CA: Mayfield Publishing Company, 1996. 5.

Guenther, Margaret. *Holy Listening*. Cambridge, MA: Cowley Publications, 1992.

———. *My Soul in Silence Waits*. Cambridge, MA: Cowley Publications. 2000.

Hall, Stephen T. "A Working Theology of Prison Ministry." *The Journal of Pastoral Care & Counseling* (58) 2004: 169–178.

Haslam, Chris. "Re: Psalm Omissions." E-mail to Lyn Fraser. 16 Aug. 2004.

Holladay, William L. *The Psalms through Three Thousand Years*. Minneapolis: Fortress Press, 1996.

Howell, James C. "The Psalms in Worship and Preaching, A Report," *Psalms and Practice*. Ed. Stephen Breck Reid. Collegeville: The Liturgical Press, 2001.

Hughes, Langston. "Harlem." *Metro*. Ed. Wendy Bishop, Katharine Haake, and Hans Ostrom. New York: Longman, 2001. 284.

Jones, L. Gregory. "Psalms of Rage." *Christian Century*. Feb. 23, 2002: 40.

Kaufman, Ivan T. "Undercut by Joy: The Sunday Lectionaries and the Psalms of Lament." *The Psalms and Other Studies on the Old Testament*. Ed. Jack C. Knight and Lawrence A. Sinclair. Cincinnati: Forward Movement Publications, 1990.

Keith, Stuart Brooks III. "Who Do You Say That I Am?" *Youth and Young Adults*. Ed. Sheryl A. Kujawa & Lois Sibley. New York: Ministries with Young People, 1995.

Kubler-Ross, Elisabeth. *On Death and Dying*. New York: Macmillan, 1969.

Lectionary for Mass (1998 USA Edition). Washington, DC: Confraternity of Christian Doctrine, 1998.

Lewis, C. S. *Reflections on the Psalms*. Glasgow: Fontana Books, 1961.

Magonet, Jonathan. *A Rabbi Reads the Psalms*. London: SCM Press Ltd., 1994.

McCann, J. Clinton, Jr. *A Theological Introduction to the Book of Psalms*. Nashville: Abingdon Press, 1993.

McCann, J. Clinton, Jr., and Howell, James C. *Preaching the Psalms*. Nashville: Abingdon Press, 2001.

Merton, Thomas. *Bread in the Wilderness*. Collegeville, MN: The Liturgical Press, 1953.

National Center for Health Statistics. U.S. Department of Health and Human Services. Center for Disease Control and Prevention. Division of Data Services, Hyattsville, MD. Work Table IV, "Deaths from Each Cause by Month, Race, and Sex: United States 1999."

A New Zealand Prayer Book. Auckland: William Collins Publishers Ltd., 1988.

Peace Lutheran Church. "Psalms." 22 Nov. 2004. <http:/www.peace-lutheranweb.com/plc/faithtoolbox/ftbpsalms4.asp>.

Power, David N. "The Eucharistic Prayer: Another Look," *New Eucharistic Prayers*. Ed. Frank C. Senn. New York: Paulist Press, 1987.

Ramshaw-Schmidt, Gail. "The Language of Eucharistic Praying," *Worship*. Sept. 1983: 419–429.

The Revised Common Lectionary. Nashville: Abingdon Press, 1992.

Shakespeare, William. Hamlet. *Responding to Literature*. Ed. Judith A. Stanford. 2nd ed. Mountain View, CA: Mayfield Publishing Company, 1996. 224.

———. "Sonnet 29." *Three Genres*. Ed. Stephen Minot. 6th ed. Upper Saddle River, NJ: Prentice Hall, 1998. 19–20.

Shepherd, Massey H., Jr. *The Psalms in Christian Worship: A Practical Guide*. Minneapolis: Augsburg Publishing House, 1976.

Soelle, Dorothee. *Suffering*. Philadelphia: Fortress Press, 1975.

Vanderbilt Divinity Library. "FAQ for the Vanderbilt Divinity Library Revised Common Lectionary." 31 Dec. 2003. 22 July 2004. <http:/divinity/lib.vanderbilt.edu/lectionary/faq.htm>.

Westermann, Claus. *The Psalms*. Minneapolis: Augsburg Publishing House, 1980.

Wiesel, Elie. *Night*. New York: Bantam Books, 1982.

Yeats. William Butler. "The Lake Isle of Innisfree." *Modern American Poetry. Modern British Poetry*. Ed. Louis Untermeyer. New York: Harcourt, Brace & World, Inc. 1962. 108.